Data Integration and Interoperability Based on CDMP

Colophon

Title:	Data Integration and Interoperability
Subtitle:	Based on CDMP
Authors:	Michel Dekker
Publisher:	Van Haren Publishing, ‘s-Hertogenbosch
ISBN Paperback:	978 94 018 1384 6
Edition: Design:	First edition, first print, October, 2025
Copyright:	Van Haren Publishing, ‘s-Hertogenbosch

For further information about Van Haren Publishing please e-mail us at: info@vanharen.net or visit our website: www.vanharen.net

Publisher about the Courseware

The Courseware was created by experts from the industry who served as the author(s) for this publication. The input for the material is based on existing publications and the experience and expertise of the author(s). The material has been revised by trainers who also have experience working with the material. Close attention was also paid to the key learning points to ensure what needs to be mastered.

The objective of the courseware is to provide maximum support to the trainer and to the student, during his or her training. The material has a modular structure and according to the author(s) has the highest success rate should the student opt for examination. The Courseware is also accredited for this reason, wherever applicable.

In order to satisfy the requirements for accreditation the material must meet certain quality standards. The structure, the use of certain terms, diagrams and references are all part of this accreditation. Additionally, the material must be made available to each student in order to obtain full accreditation. To optimally support the trainer and the participant of the training assignments, practice exams and results are provided with the material.

Direct reference to advised literature is also regularly covered in the sheets so that students can find additional information concerning a particular topic. The decision to leave out notes pages from the Courseware was to encourage students to take notes throughout the material. Although the courseware is complete, the possibility that the trainer deviates from the structure of the sheets or chooses to not refer to all the sheets or commands does exist. The student always has the possibility to cover these topics and go through them on their own time. It is recommended to follow the structure of the courseware and publications for maximum exam preparation.

The courseware and the recommended literature are the perfect combination to learn and understand the theory.

-- Van Haren Publishing

Other publications BY Van Haren Publishing

Van Haren Publishing (VHP) specializes in titles on Best Practices, methods, frameworks and standards within four domains:
- IT Management
- Architecture (Enterprise and IT)
- Business Management and
- Project Management

Van Haren Publishing is publishing on behalf of leading organizations and companies: Agile Consortium, World Commerce and Contracting, IAOP, IPMA World, KNVI, PMI-NL, NLAIC and The Open Group.

Van Haren Publishing is part of the Van Haren Group and additional to the book publishing also provides the following services: accredited training materials and e-learning through Van Haren Learning Solutions, as well as independent professional certification via examination through Van Haren Certify.

Topics are (per domain):

IT Management	IT Service Management	FitSM, ISM®, ISO/IEC20000, IT4IT®, ITIL®, VerISM®, SAF, TRIM, XLA®
	Data Management	Data literacy, Data visualization, DMBOK
	IT Asset Management	HAM, ITAM, SAM
	IT Security Management	BIO, ISO/IEC27001, NIS2
	Test Management	CTAP
	Application Management	ASL
	Other	eCF, IT-CMF, Scrum
Project Management	Project Management	Half Double, ICB, ISO/IEC21500, P3.express, PM2, PMBOK Guide, Praxis, PRINCE2
	Agile	Agile, Agile PM
	Other	PMO
Business Management	Operations Management	Lean, Lean Six Sigma, OBM, OMC, RASCI
	Contract Management	CATS CM, CATS RVM, IACCM World
	Business Information Management	BiSL, DID
	Artificial Intelligence	AI, Generative AI
	Outsourcing	OPBOK
Enterprise Architecture	Enterprise Architecture	BIAN, TOGAF
	Modeling	ArchiMate, BPMN
	Software Architecture	ISAQB
	Other	Open Agile Architecture

For the latest information on VHP publications, visit our website: www.vanharen.net.

Table of Content

Self-Reflection of understanding Diagram

'What you do not measure, you cannot control." – Tom Peters

Fill in this diagram to self-evaluate your understanding of the material. This is an evaluation of how well you know the material and how well you understand it. In order to pass the exam successfully you should be aiming to reach the higher end of Level 3. If you really want to become a pro, then you should be aiming for Level 4. Your overall level of understanding will naturally follow the learning curve. So, it's important to keep track of where you are at each point of the training and address any areas of difficulty.

Based on where you are within the Self-Reflection of Understanding diagram you can evaluate the progress of your own training.

Level of Understanding	Before Training (Pre-knowledge)	Training Part 1 (1st Half)	raining Part 2 (2nd Half)	After studying / reading the book	After exercises and the Practice exam
Level 4 ***I can explain the content and apply it .***					
Level 3 I get it! ***I am right where I am supposed to be.***					Ready for the exam!
Level 2 ***I almost have it but could use more practice.***					
Level 1 ***I am learning but don't quite get it yet.***					

(Self-Reflection of Understanding Diagram)

Write down the problem areas that you are still having difficulty with so that you can consolidate them yourself, or with your trainer. After you have had a look at these, then you should evaluate to see if you now have a better understanding of where you actually are on the learning curve.

Troubleshooting

	Problem areas:	***Topic:***
Part 1		
Part 2		
You have gone through the book and studied.		
You have answered the questions and done the practice exam.		

Data Integration and Interoperability

Effective Data Foundation

Not-for-profit collective, which enables **professionals** to **leverage data** to make **sustainable business decisions**

 2

Effective Data Foundation
DATA
Analysis / Literacy / Management / Visualization
© Van Haren Publishing
3

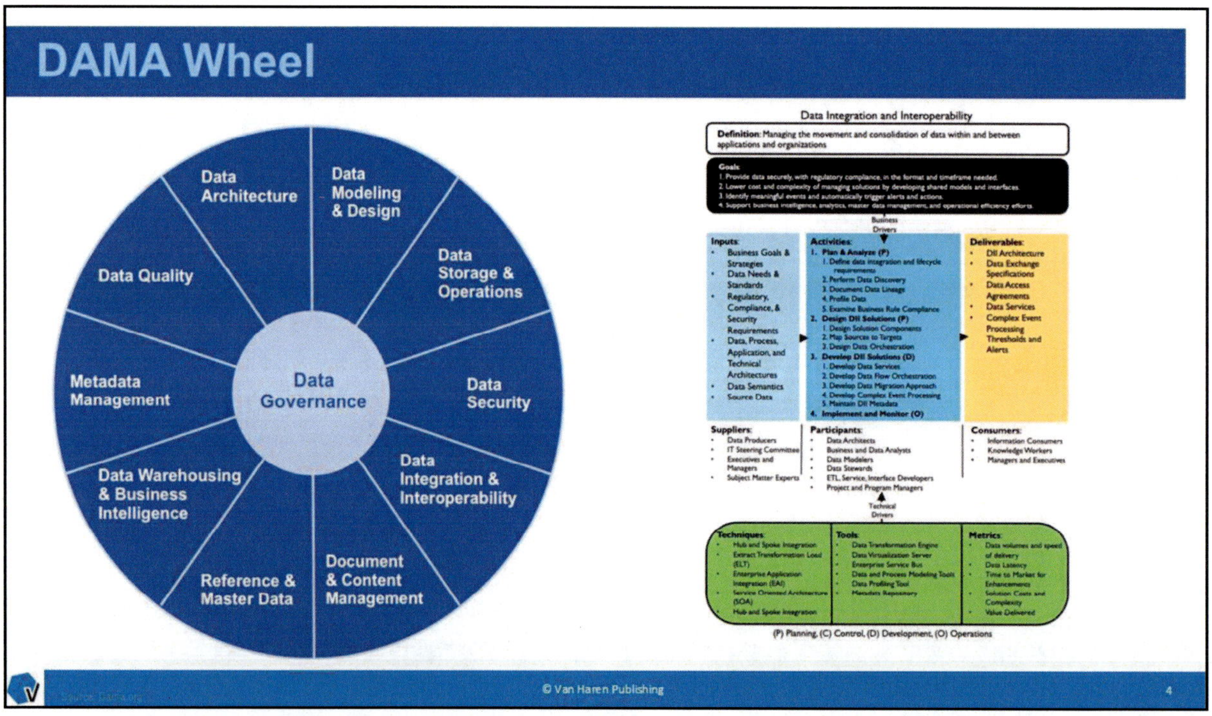
DAMA Wheel
Data Architecture
Data Modeling & Design
Data Storage & Operations
Data Security
Data Integration & Interoperability
Document & Content Management
Reference & Master Data
Data Warehousing & Business Intelligence
Metadata Management
Data Quality
Data Governance
Data Integration and Interoperability
Definition: Managing the movement and consolidation of data within and between applications and organizations
Goals:
1. Provide data securely, with regulatory compliance, in the format and timeframe needed.
2. Lower cost and complexity of managing solutions by developing shared models and interfaces.
3. Identify meaningful events and automatically trigger alerts and actions.
4. Support business intelligence, analytics, master data management, and operational efficiency efforts.
Business Drivers
Inputs:
Business Goals & Strategies
Data Needs & Standards
Regulatory, Compliance, & Security Requirements
Data, Process, Application, and Technical Architectures
Data Semantics
Source Data
Activities:
1. Plan & Analyze (P)
2. Design DII Solutions (P)
3. Develop DII Solutions (D)
4. Implement and Monitor (O)
Deliverables:
DII Architecture
Data Exchange Specifications
Data Access Agreements
Data Services
Complex Event Processing Thresholds and Alerts
Suppliers:
Data Producers
IT Steering Committee
Executives and Managers
Subject Matter Experts
Participants:
Data Architects
Business and Data Analysts
Data Modelers
Data Stewards
ETL, Service, Interface Developers
Project and Program Managers
Consumers:
Information Consumers
Knowledge Workers
Managers and Executives
Technical Drivers
Techniques:
Tools:
Metrics:
(P) Planning, (C) Control, (D) Development, (O) Operations
© Van Haren Publishing
4

Certification
ASSOCIATE
PRACTITIONER
MASTER
FELLOW
CDMP Associate
CDMP Practitioner
CDMP Master
CDMP Fellow
Membership
Central
Industry experience
6 months > 5 years
2 years - 10 years
Minimum 10 years^
25 years plus
Requirements
60% pass Data Management Fundamentals exam
70% pass in Data Management Fundamentals exam and 70% pass in 2 specialist exams
80% pass in Data Management Fundamentals exam and 80% pass in 2 specialist exams
Globally recognised & respected thought leadership
Significant contribution to Data Management profession
CDMP Master
Contribution to CDMP & DMBOK
By nomination
© Van Haren Publishing
5

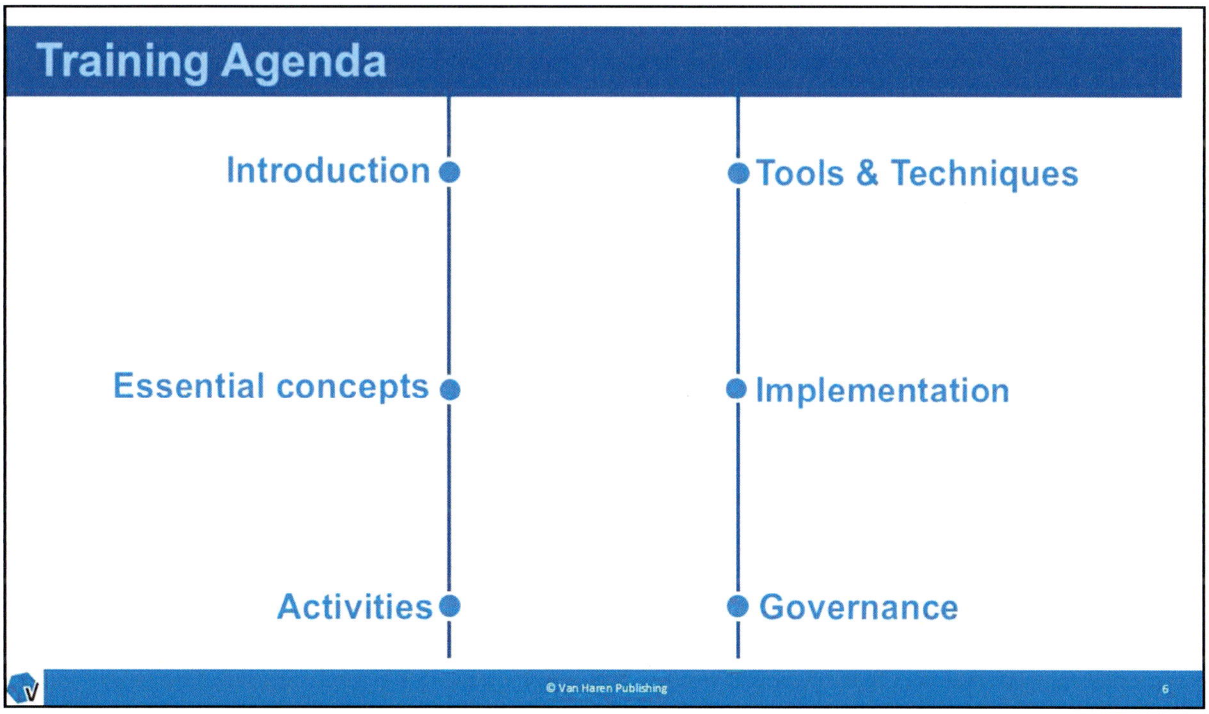
Training Agenda
Introduction
Essential concepts
Activities
Tools & Techniques
Implementation
Governance
© Van Haren Publishing
6

Introduction

*Data integration is the combination of technical and business processes used to combine data from **disparate sources into meaningful and valuable information***

William McKnight

Definition

Managing the **movement** and **consolidation** of data **within** and **between** applications and organizations

Data Integration
consolidates data into consistent forms, either physical or virtual

Data Interoperability
ability for multiple systems to communicate

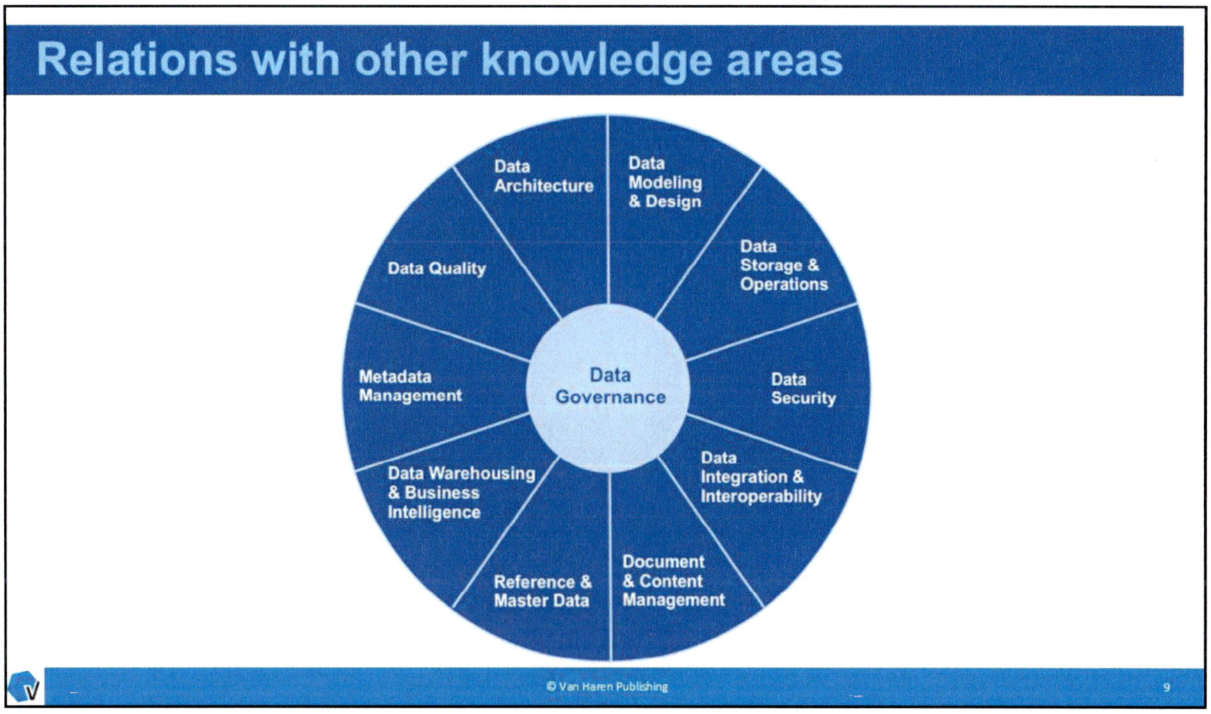
Relations with other knowledge areas
Data Architecture
Data Modeling & Design
Data Storage & Operations
Data Quality
Metadata Management
Data Governance
Data Security
Data Integration & Interoperability
Data Warehousing & Business Intelligence
Reference & Master Data
Document & Content Management
© Van Haren Publishing
9

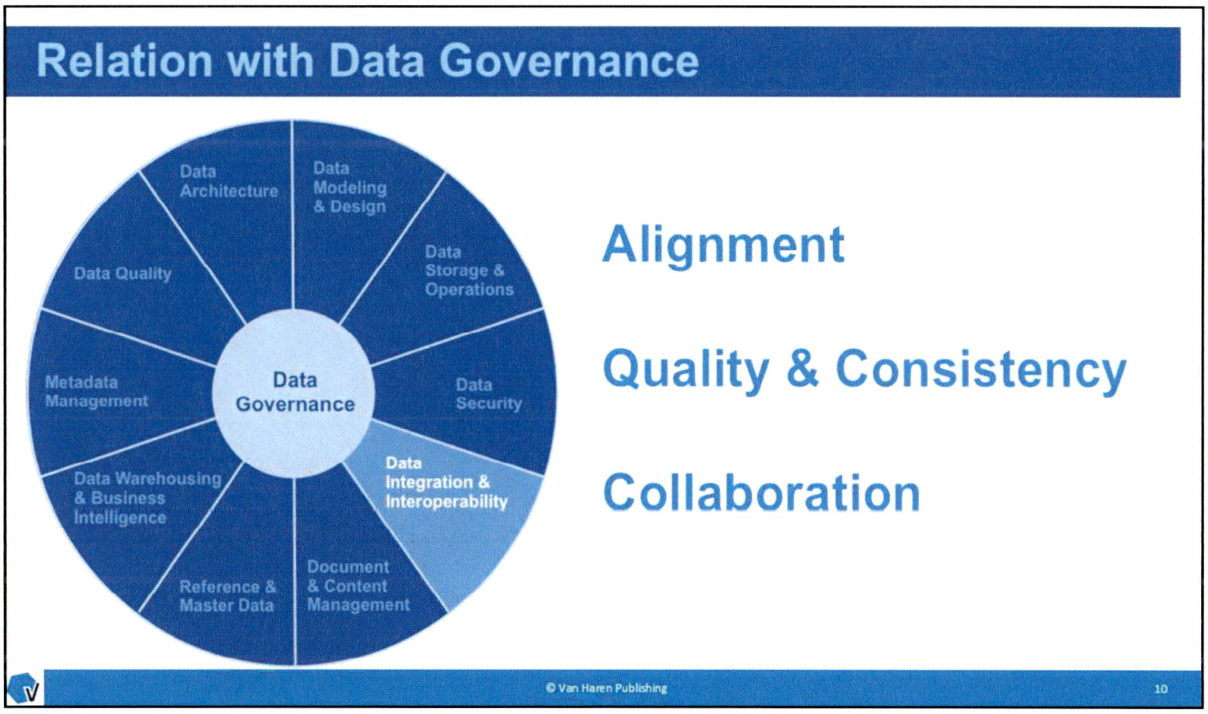
Relation with Data Governance
Data Architecture
Data Modeling & Design
Data Storage & Operations
Data Quality
Metadata Management
Data Governance
Data Security
Data Integration & Interoperability
Data Warehousing & Business Intelligence
Reference & Master Data
Document & Content Management
Alignment
Quality & Consistency
Collaboration
© Van Haren Publishing
10

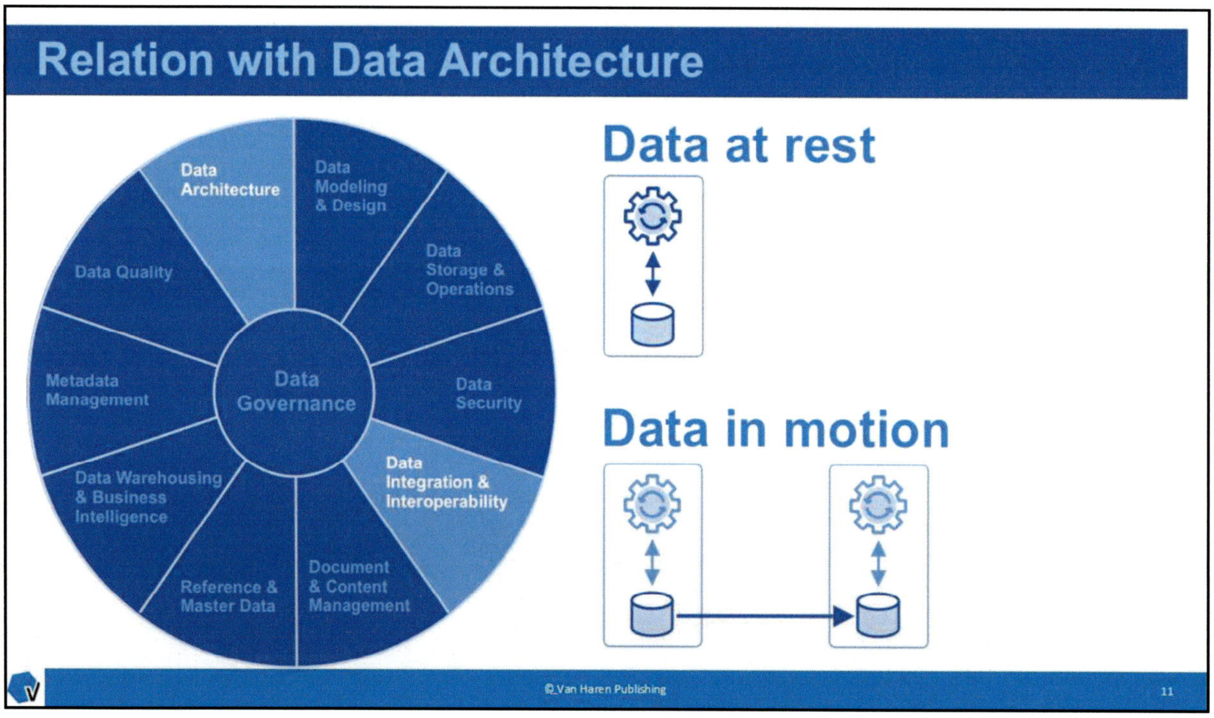
Relation with Data Architecture
Data Architecture
Data Modeling & Design
Data Storage & Operations
Data Security
Data Integration & Interoperability
Document & Content Management
Reference & Master Data
Data Warehousing & Business Intelligence
Metadata Management
Data Quality
Data Governance
Data at rest
Data in motion
© Van Haren Publishing
11

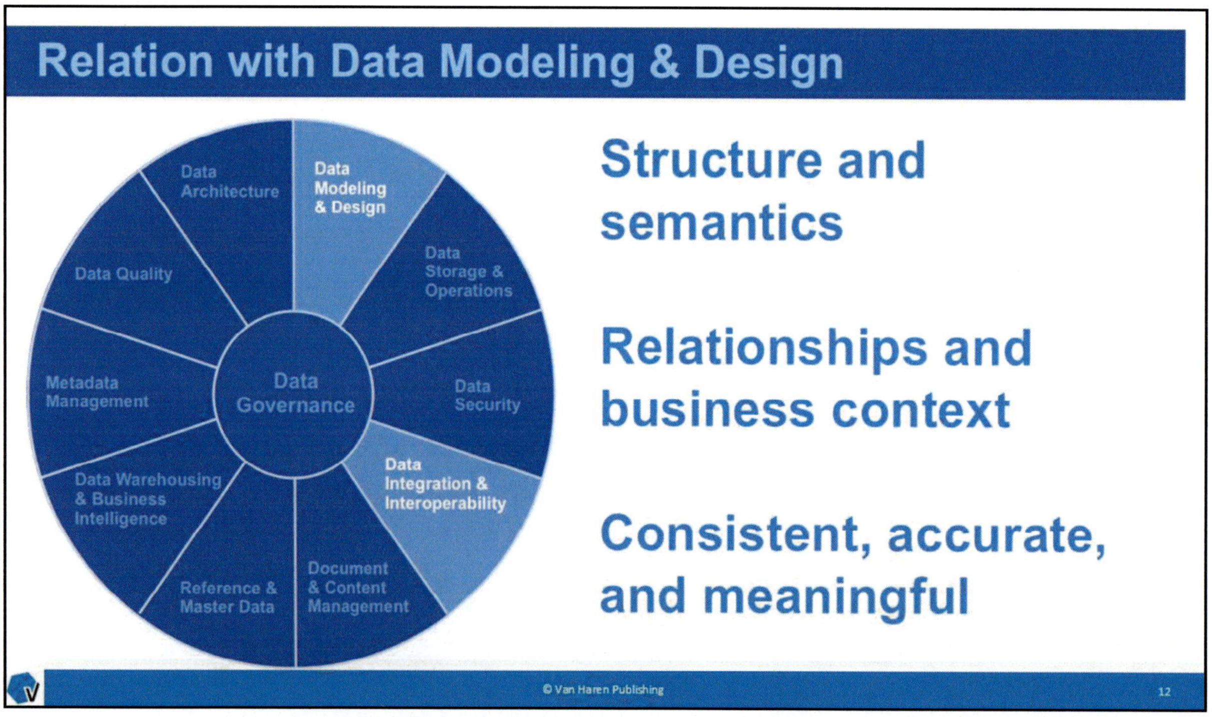
Relation with Data Modeling & Design
Data Architecture
Data Modeling & Design
Data Storage & Operations
Data Security
Data Integration & Interoperability
Document & Content Management
Reference & Master Data
Data Warehousing & Business Intelligence
Metadata Management
Data Quality
Data Governance
Structure and semantics
Relationships and business context
Consistent, accurate, and meaningful
© Van Haren Publishing
12

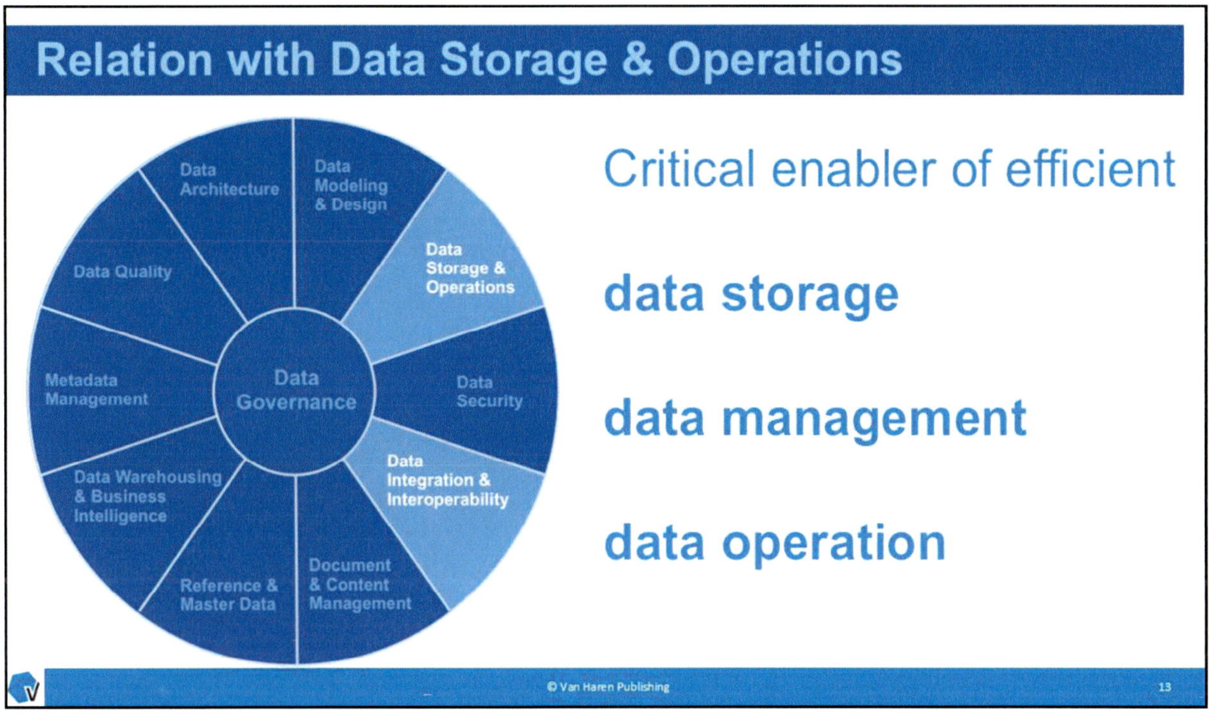
Relation with Data Storage & Operations
Data Architecture
Data Modeling & Design
Data Storage & Operations
Data Quality
Data Governance
Data Security
Metadata Management
Data Integration & Interoperability
Data Warehousing & Business Intelligence
Reference & Master Data
Document & Content Management
Critical enabler of efficient
data storage
data management
data operation
© Van Haren Publishing
13

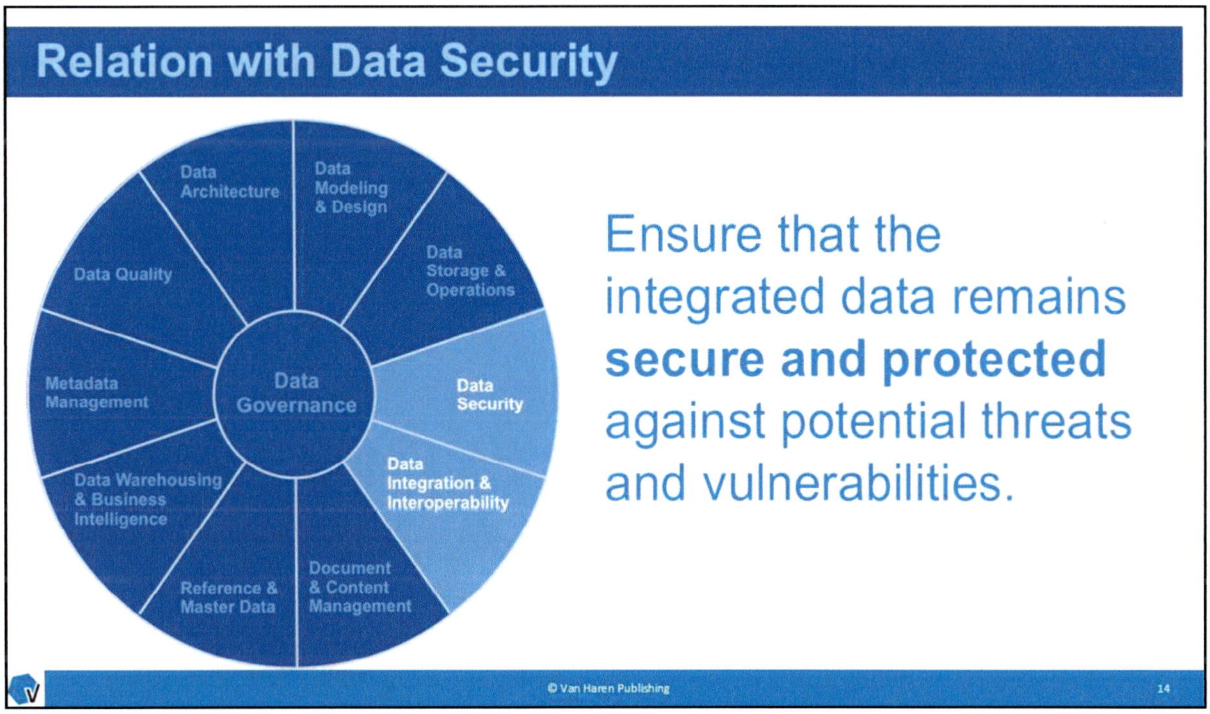
Relation with Data Security
Data Architecture
Data Modeling & Design
Data Storage & Operations
Data Quality
Data Governance
Data Security
Metadata Management
Data Integration & Interoperability
Data Warehousing & Business Intelligence
Reference & Master Data
Document & Content Management
Ensure that the integrated data remains secure and protected against potential threats and vulnerabilities.
© Van Haren Publishing
14

Relation with Document & Content Management

integrate **structured** and **unstructured** data

Lifecycle management

 15

Relation with Reference & Master Data

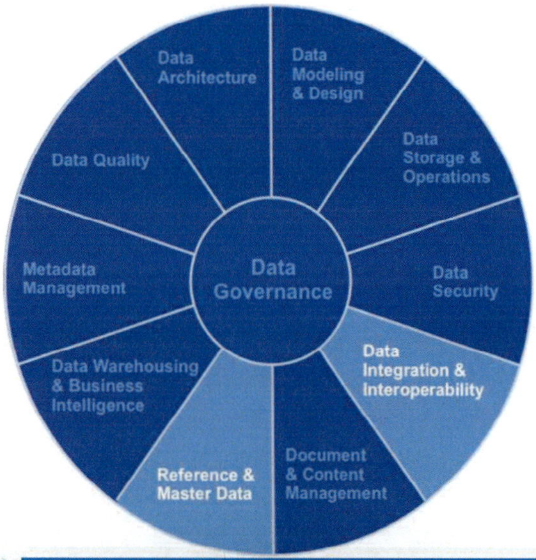

Without DII any form of Reference or Master Data is **challenging**

Robust Reference & Master Data **facilitates** data integration efforts

 16

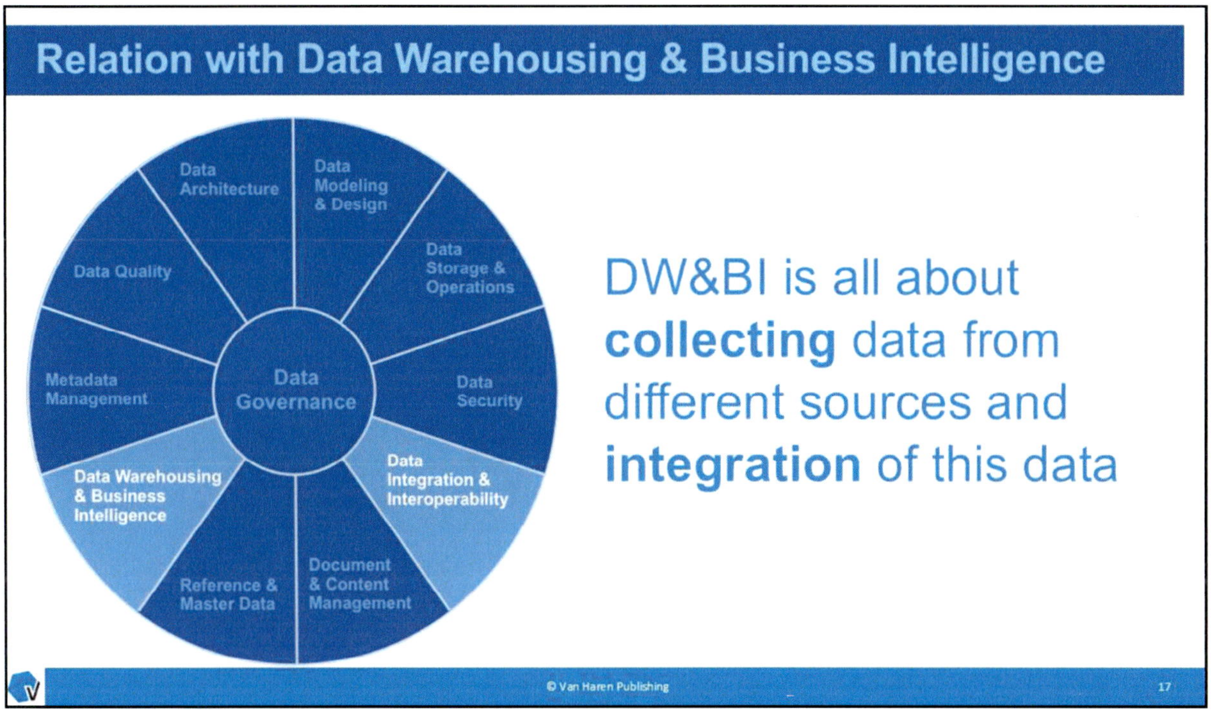
Relation with Data Warehousing & Business Intelligence
Data Architecture
Data Modeling & Design
Data Storage & Operations
Data Security
Data Integration & Interoperability
Document & Content Management
Reference & Master Data
Data Warehousing & Business Intelligence
Metadata Management
Data Quality
Data Governance
DW&BI is all about **collecting** data from different sources and **integration** of this data
© Van Haren Publishing
17

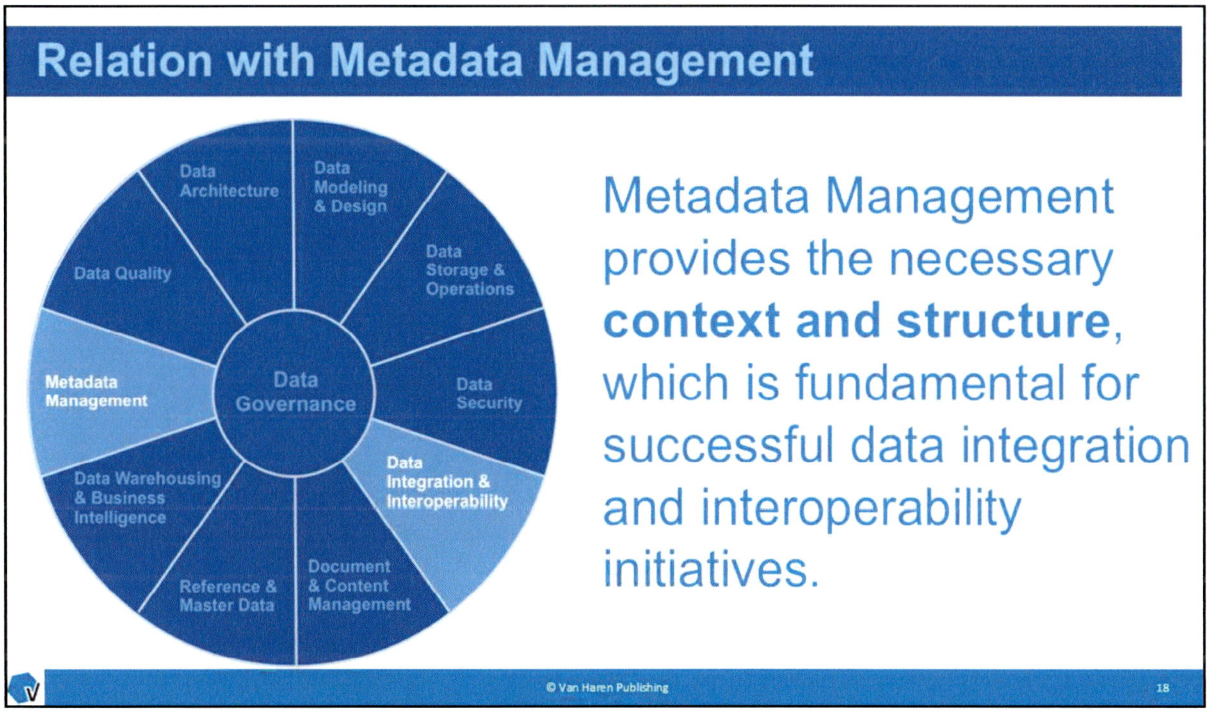
Relation with Metadata Management
Data Architecture
Data Modeling & Design
Data Storage & Operations
Data Security
Data Integration & Interoperability
Document & Content Management
Reference & Master Data
Data Warehousing & Business Intelligence
Metadata Management
Data Quality
Data Governance
Metadata Management provides the necessary **context and structure**, which is fundamental for successful data integration and interoperability initiatives.
© Van Haren Publishing
18

Relation with Data Quality

data quality management is crucial for ensuring that the integrated data is **trustworthy** and **fit for** its intended **use**.

Business Drivers

Manage data movement **efficiently**

Manage the **cost** of support of complex solutions

Comply with standards and regulations

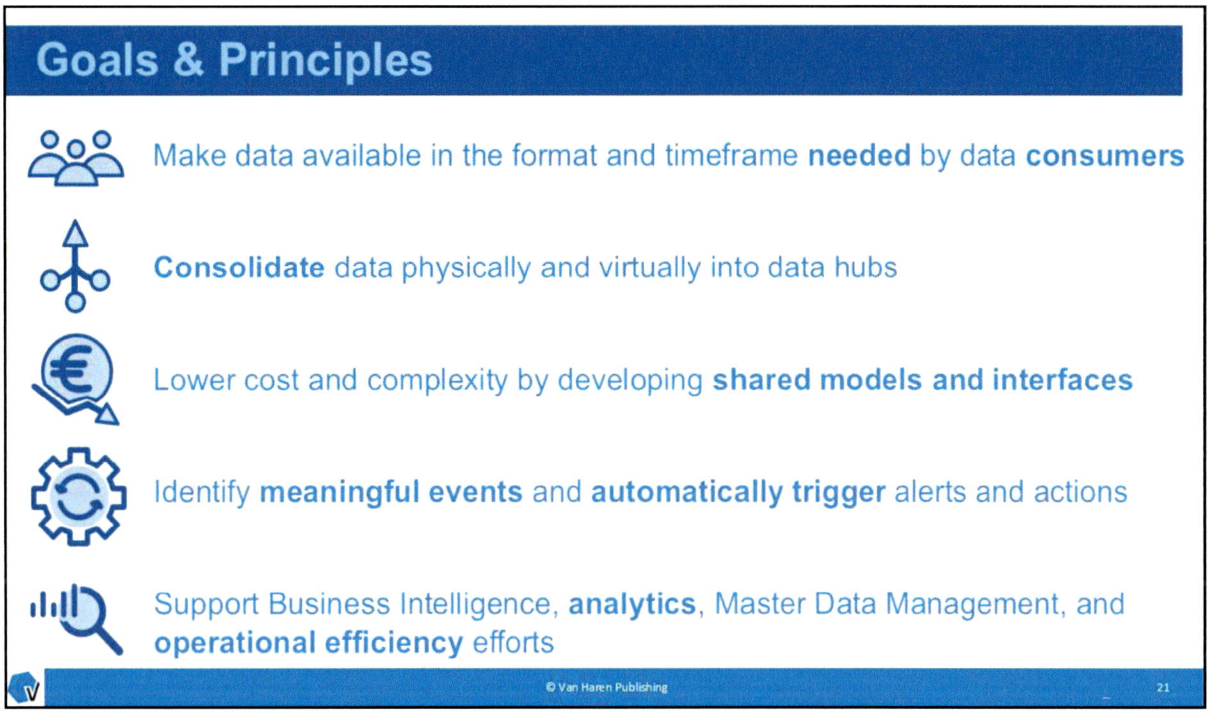
Goals & Principles
Make data available in the format and timeframe **needed** by data **consumers**
Consolidate data physically and virtually into data hubs
Lower cost and complexity by developing **shared models and interfaces**
Identify **meaningful events** and **automatically trigger** alerts and actions
Support Business Intelligence, **analytics**, Master Data Management, and **operational efficiency** efforts
© Van Haren Publishing
21

Goals & Principles
Enterprise perspective in design
Balance local data needs with enterprise data needs
Ensure business accountability
© Van Haren Publishing
22

Essential Concepts
© Van Haren Publishing
23

Extract, Transform, Load
IMO MAX
© Van Haren Publishing
24

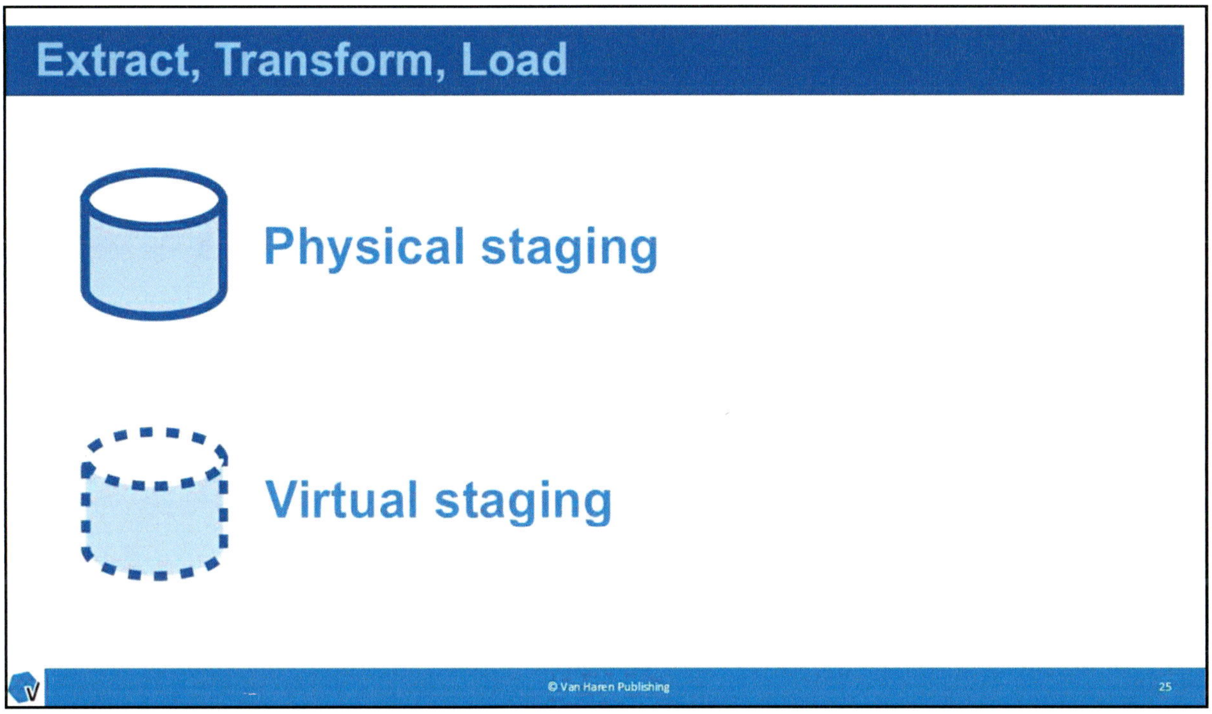
Extract, Transform, Load
Physical staging
Virtual staging
© Van Haren Publishing
25

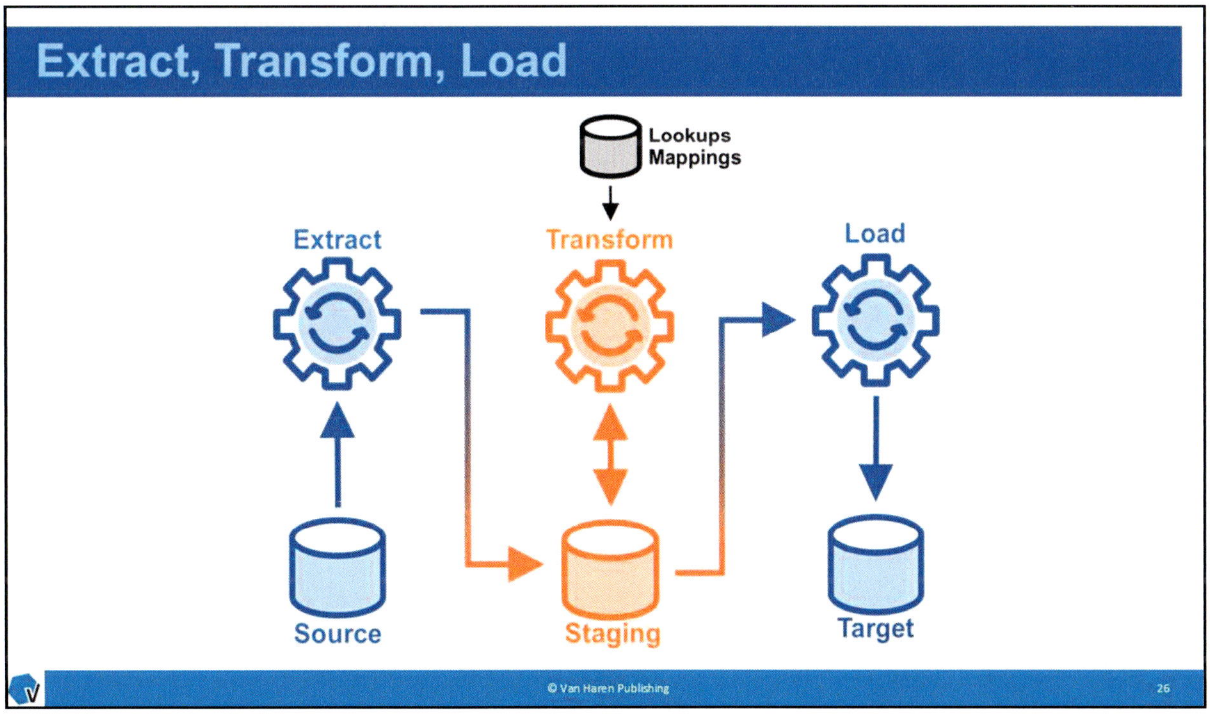
Extract, Transform, Load
Lookups
Mappings
Extract
Transform
Load
Source
Staging
Target
© Van Haren Publishing
26

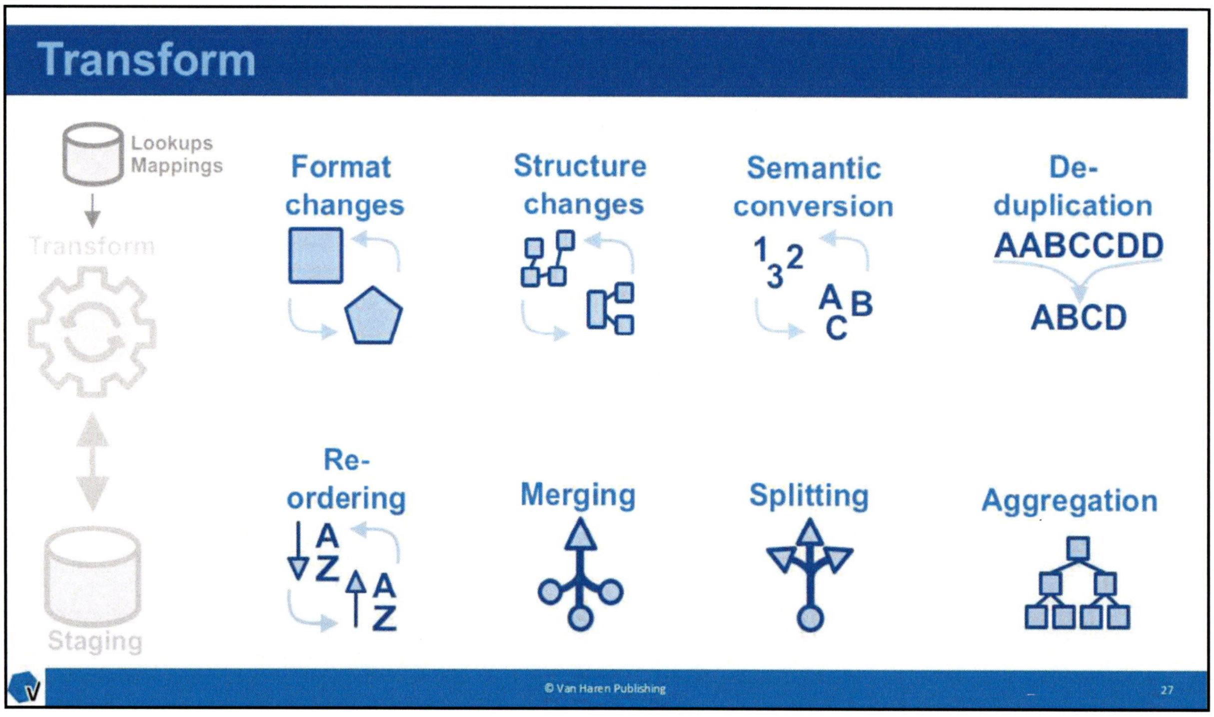
Transform
Lookups
Mappings
Transform
Staging
Format
changes
Structure
changes
Semantic
conversion
1
3
2
A
B
C
De-
duplication
AABCCDD
ABCD
Re-
ordering
A
Z
A
Z
Merging
Splitting
Aggregation
© Van Haren Publishing
27

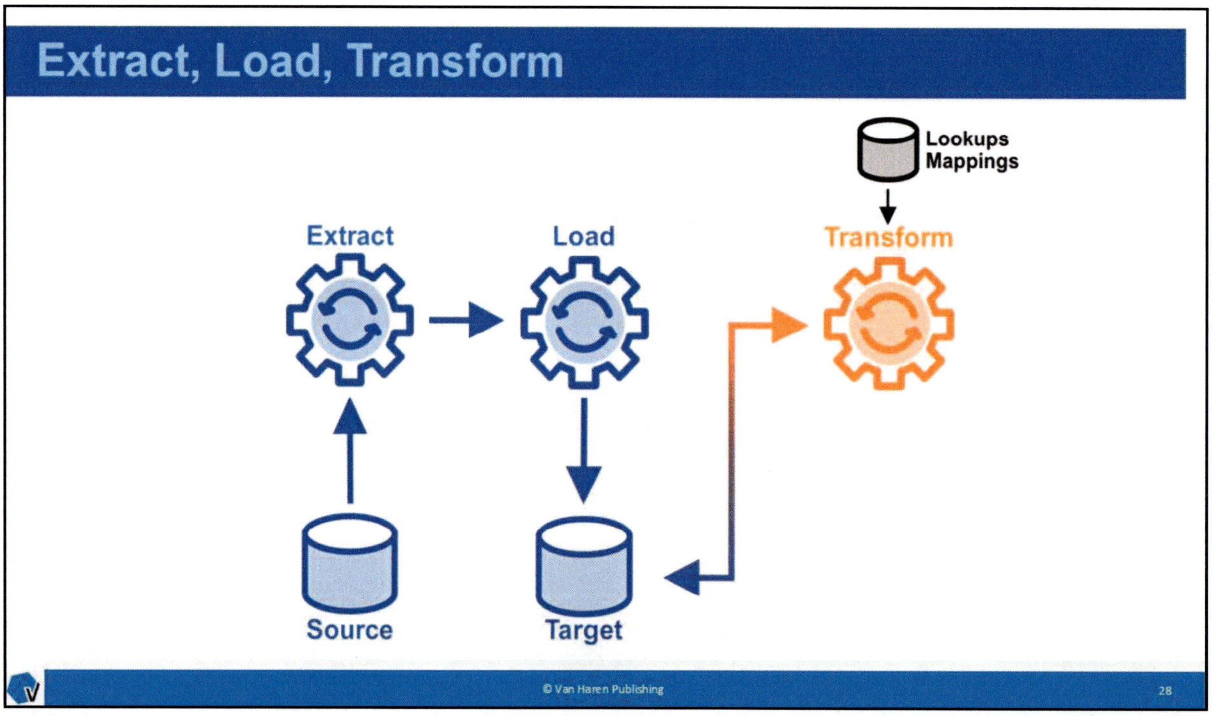
Extract, Load, Transform
Lookups
Mappings
Extract
Load
Transform
Source
Target
© Van Haren Publishing
28

ETL and ELT considerations

	ETL	ELT
Pros	Structured Processing	Scalabilty
	Data Quality	Real-time Data
	Historical Data Transformation	Simple Architecture
Cons	Latency	Raw Data Load
	Complexity	Data Quality
	Mainly Batch Processing	Dependency on DWH

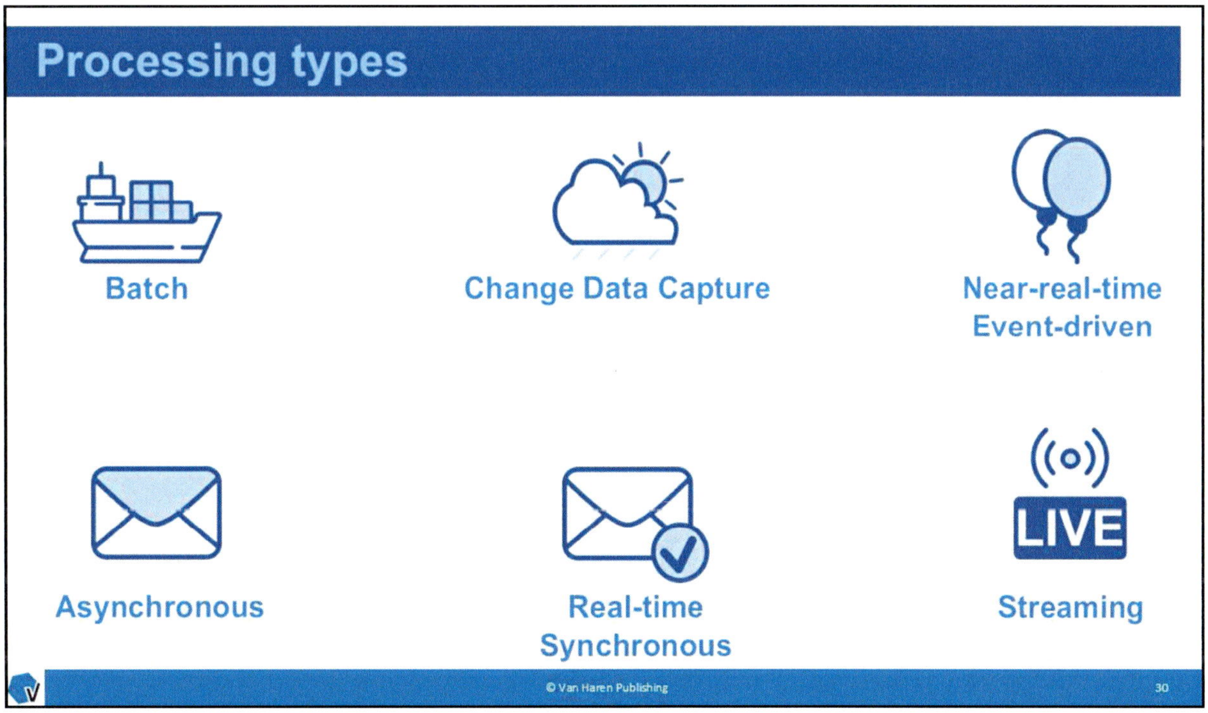

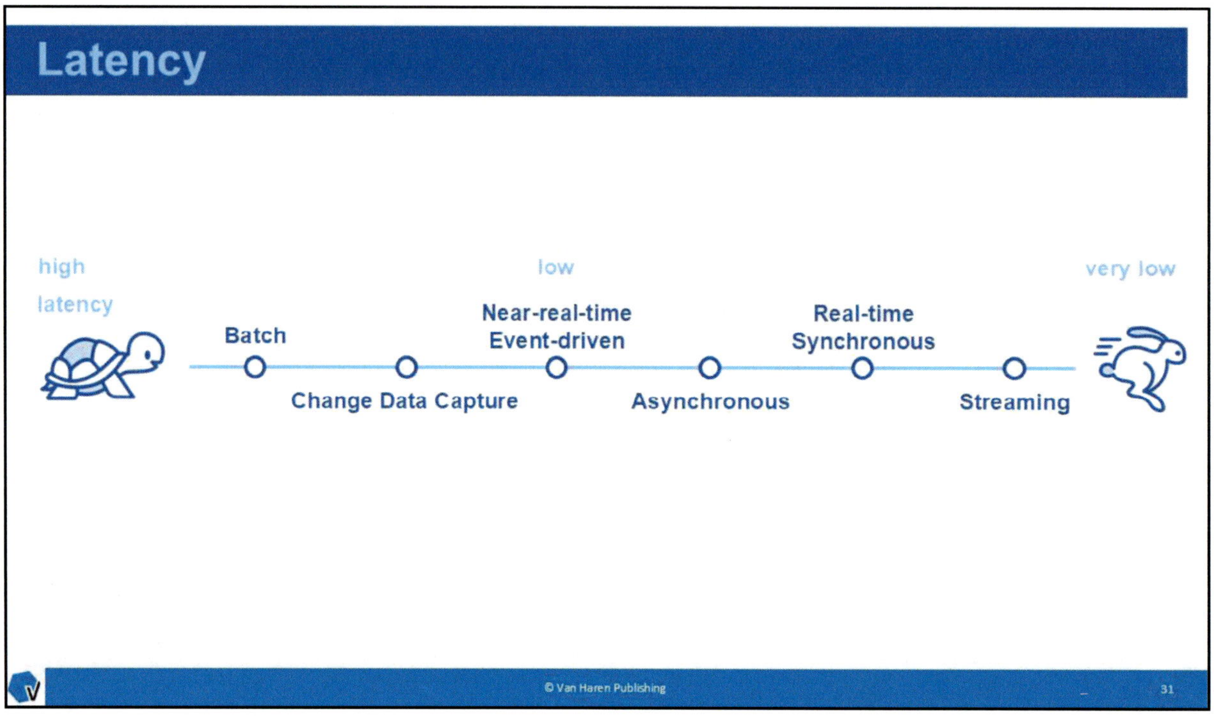
Latency
high
latency
low
very low
Batch
Change Data Capture
Near-real-time
Event-driven
Asynchronous
Real-time
Synchronous
Streaming
© Van Haren Publishing
31

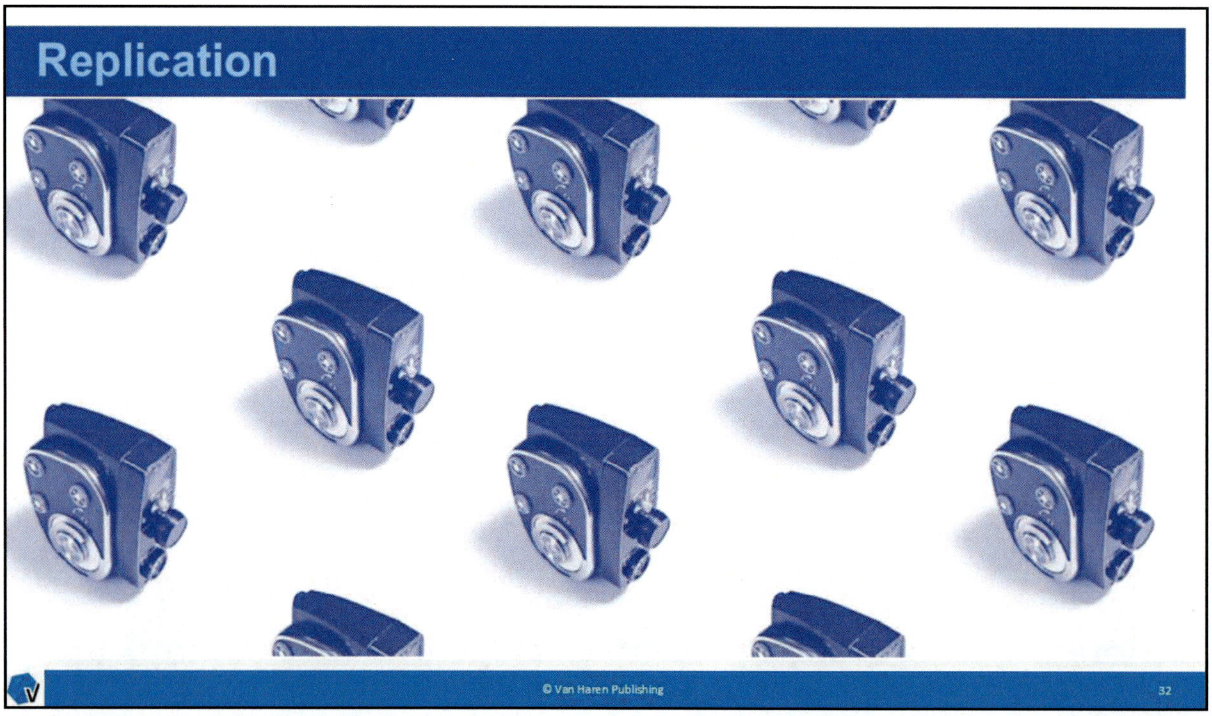
Replication
© Van Haren Publishing
32

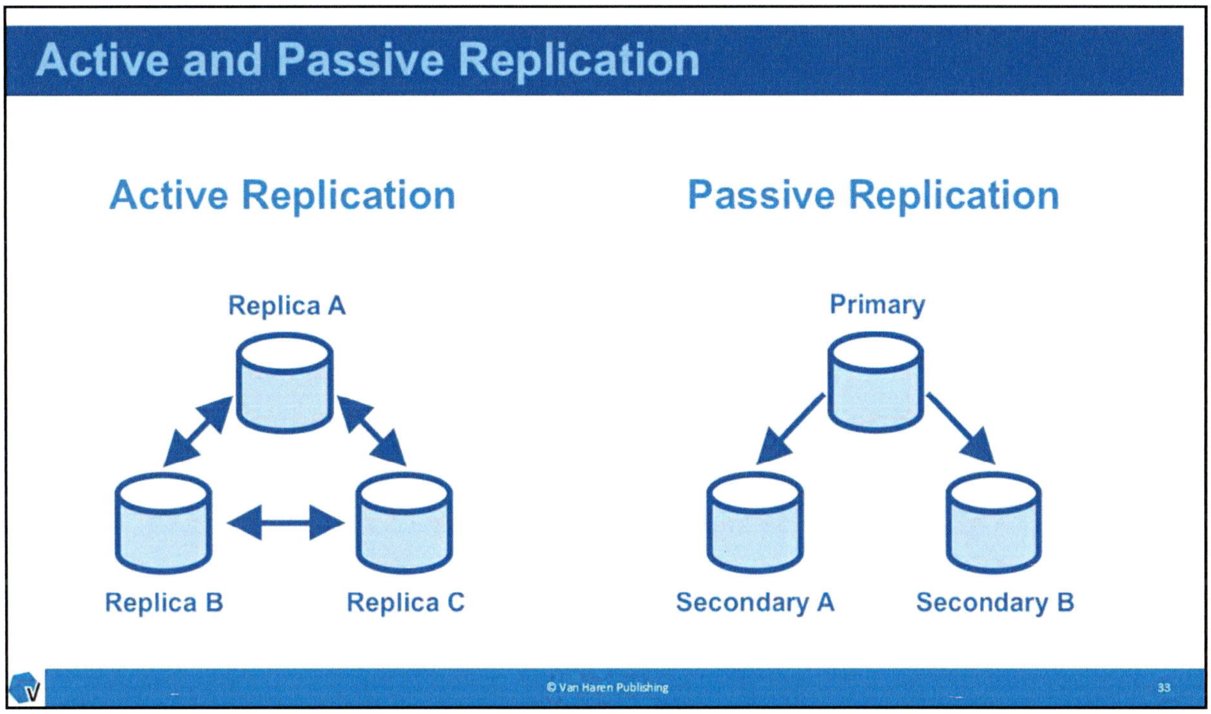
Active and Passive Replication
Active Replication
Replica A
Replica B
Replica C
Passive Replication
Primary
Secondary A
Secondary B
© Van Haren Publishing
33

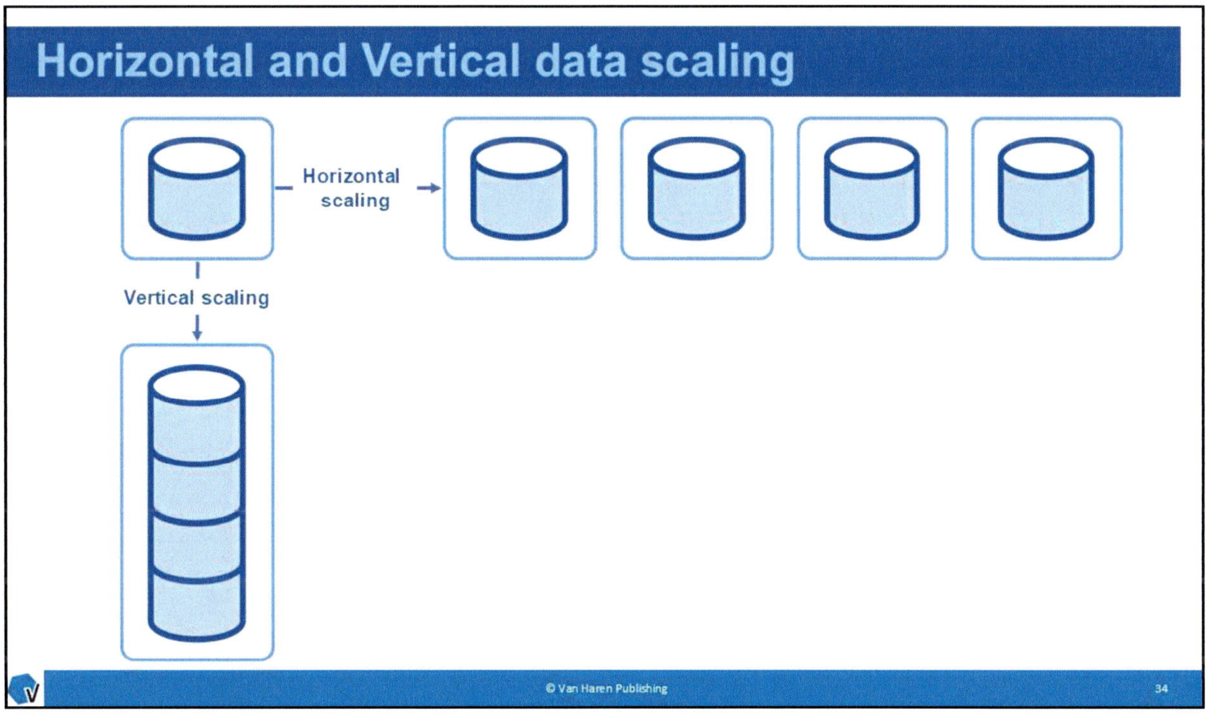
Horizontal and Vertical data scaling
Horizontal scaling
Vertical scaling
© Van Haren Publishing
34

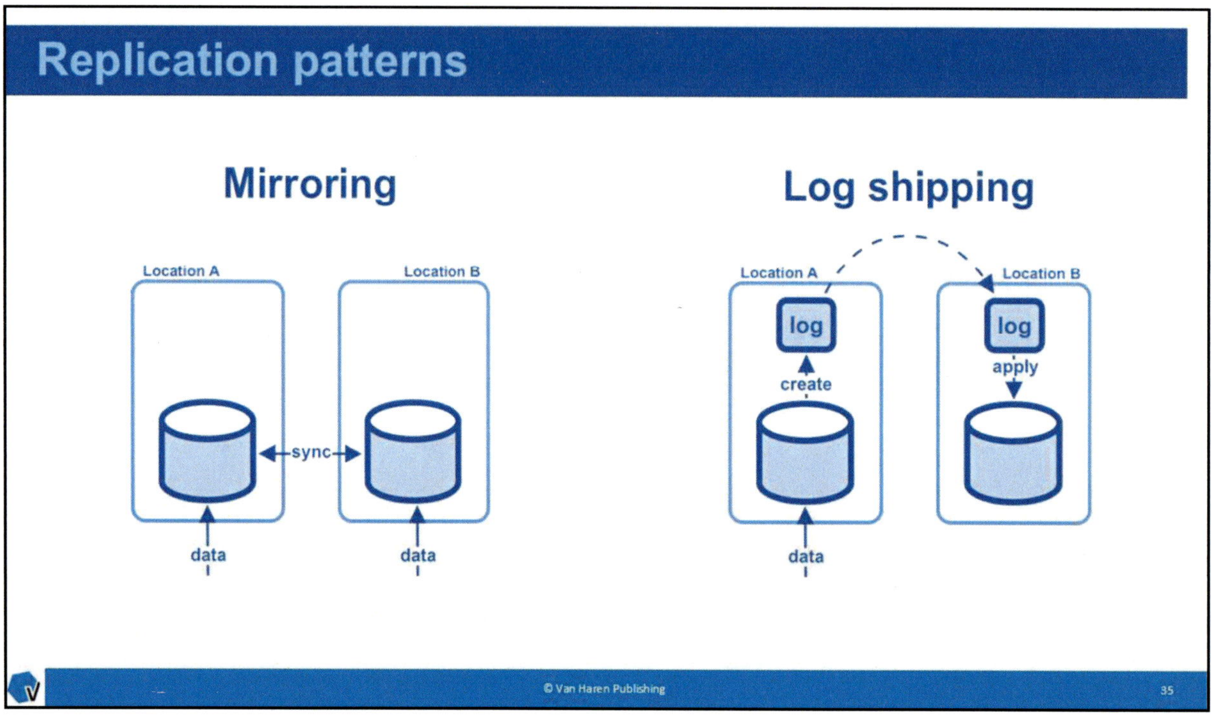
Replication patterns
Mirroring
Location A
Location B
sync
data
data
Log shipping
Location A
Location B
log
create
log
apply
data
© Van Haren Publishing
35

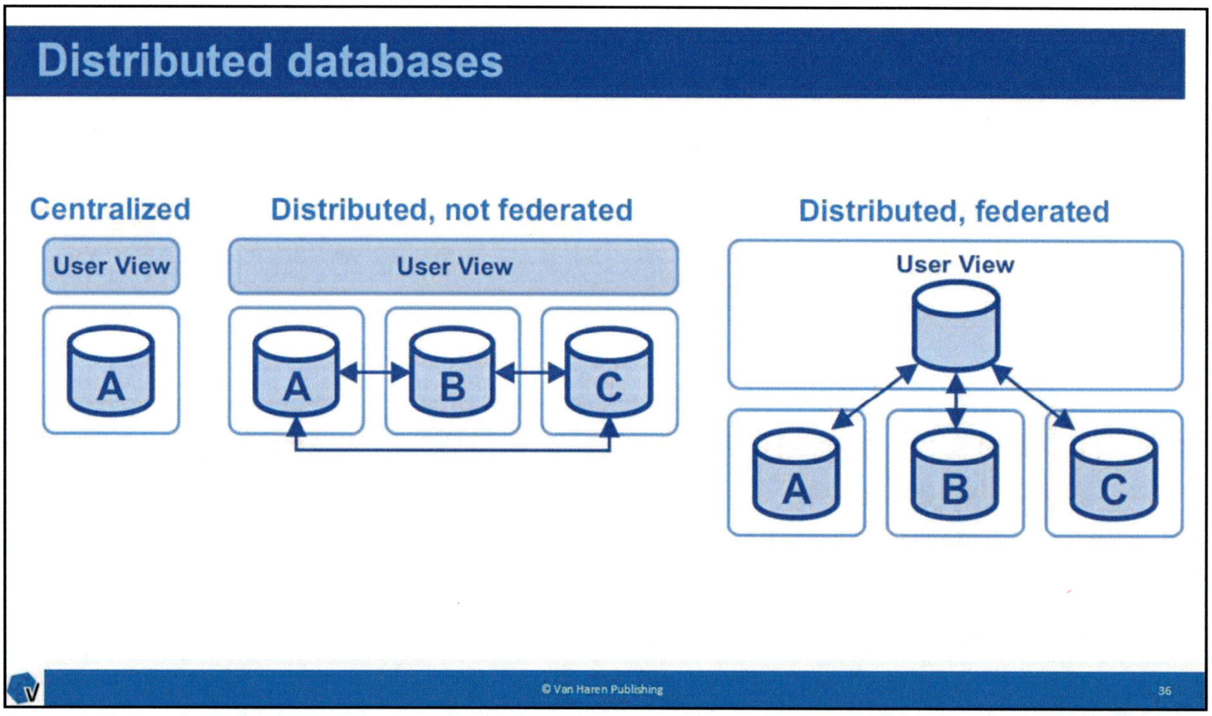
Distributed databases
Centralized
User View
A
Distributed, not federated
User View
A
B
C
Distributed, federated
User View
A
B
C
© Van Haren Publishing
36

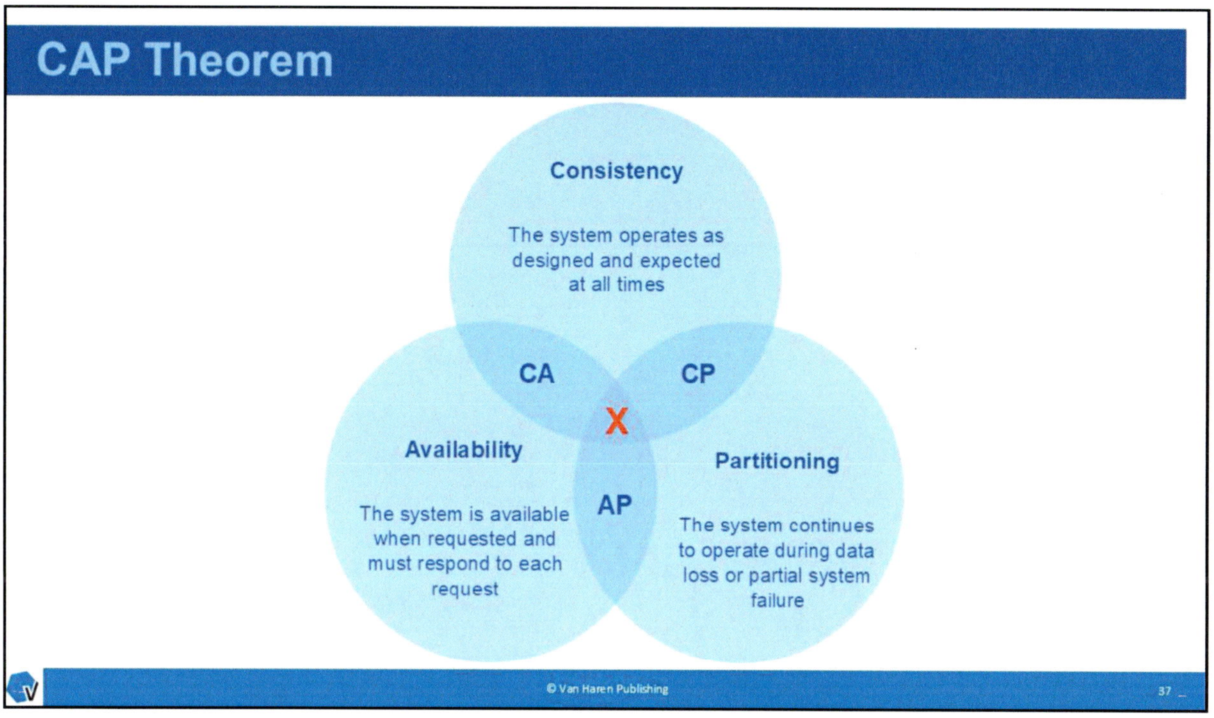
CAP Theorem
Consistency
The system operates as designed and expected at all times
CA
CP
X
Availability
The system is available when requested and must respond to each request
AP
Partitioning
The system continues to operate during data loss or partial system failure
© Van Haren Publishing
37

Archiving
Cost Efficiency
Compliance & Regulations
Resource Optimization
Disaster Recovery
© Van Haren Publishing
38

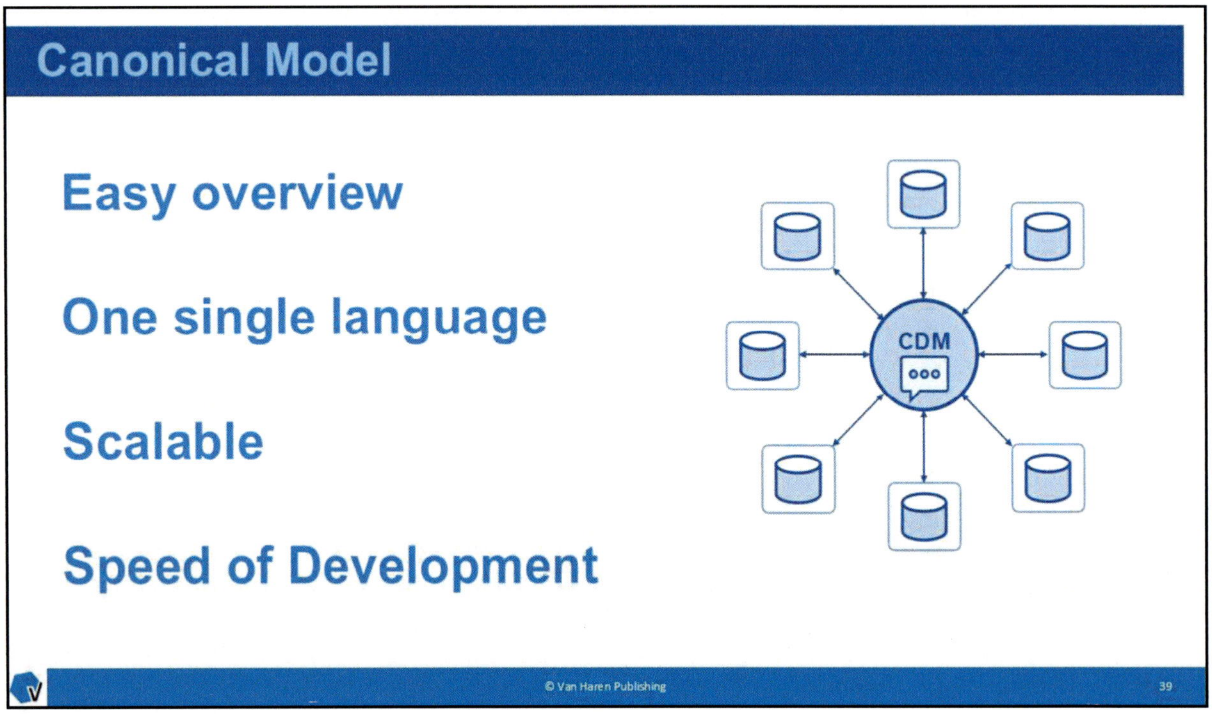
Canonical Model
Easy overview
One single language
Scalable
Speed of Development
CDM
© Van Haren Publishing
39

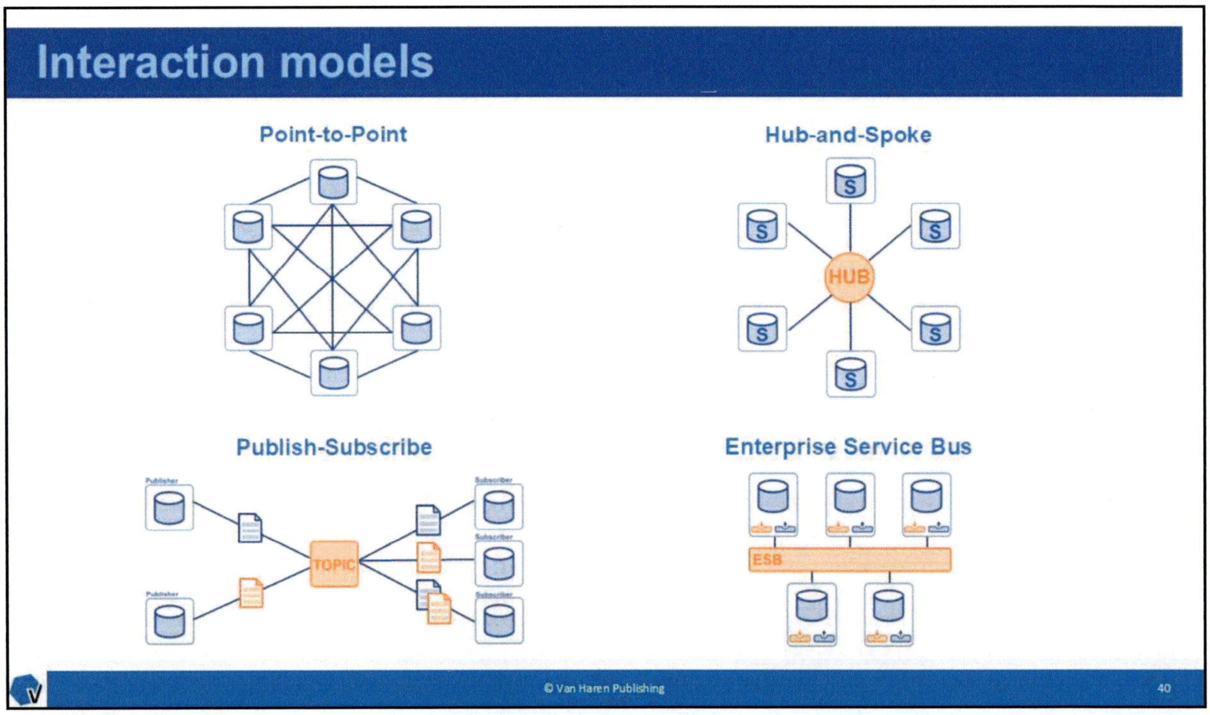
Interaction models
Point-to-Point
Hub-and-Spoke
HUB
S
Publish-Subscribe
TOPIC
Enterprise Service Bus
ESB
© Van Haren Publishing
40

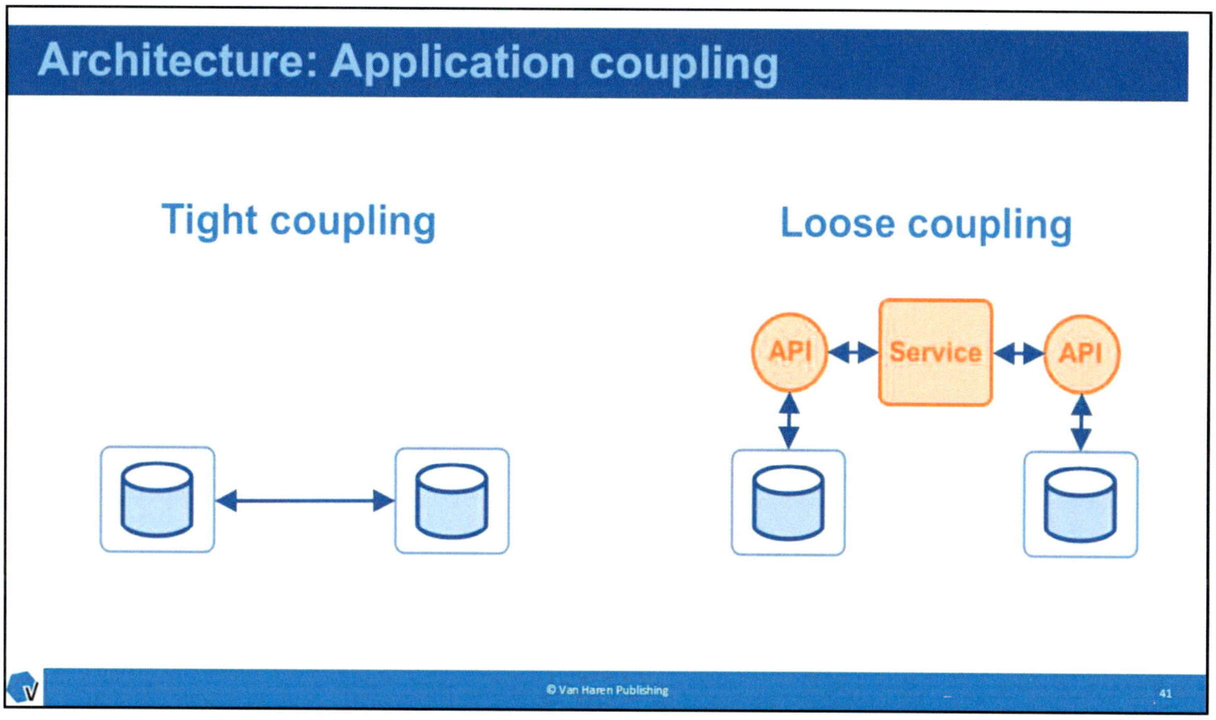
Architecture: Application coupling
Tight coupling
Loose coupling
API
Service
API
© Van Haren Publishing
41

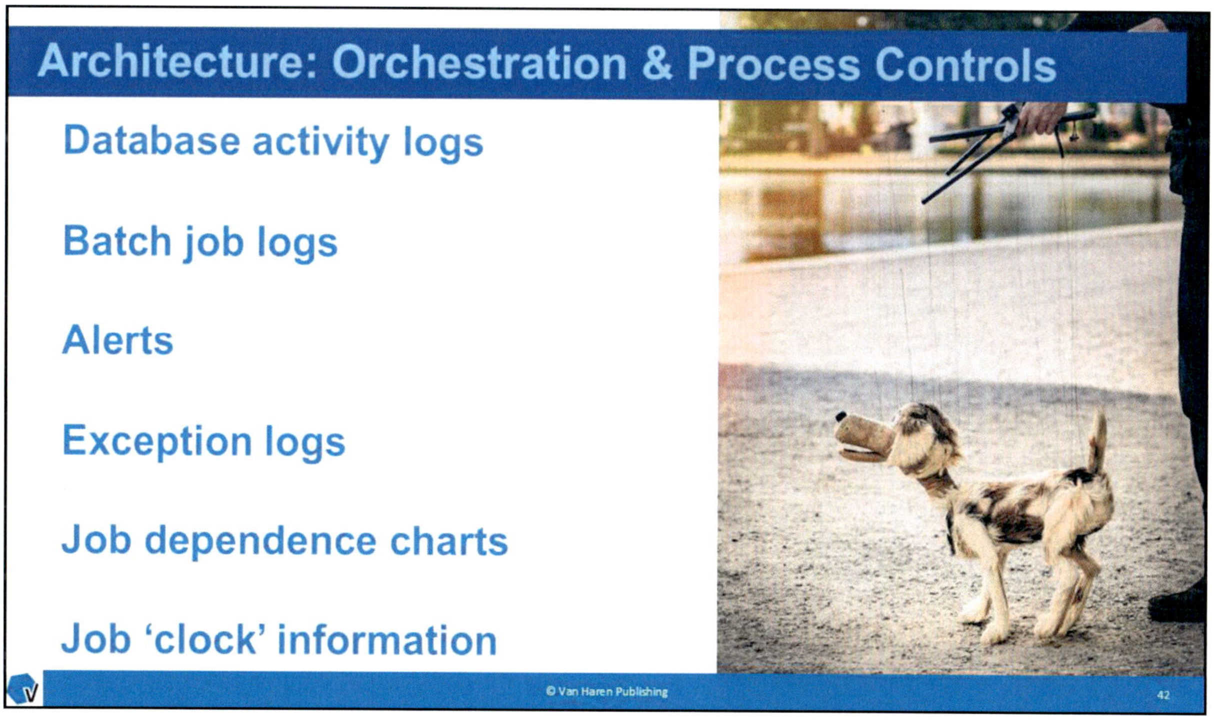
Architecture: Orchestration & Process Controls
Database activity logs
Batch job logs
Alerts
Exception logs
Job dependence charts
Job 'clock' information
© Van Haren Publishing
42

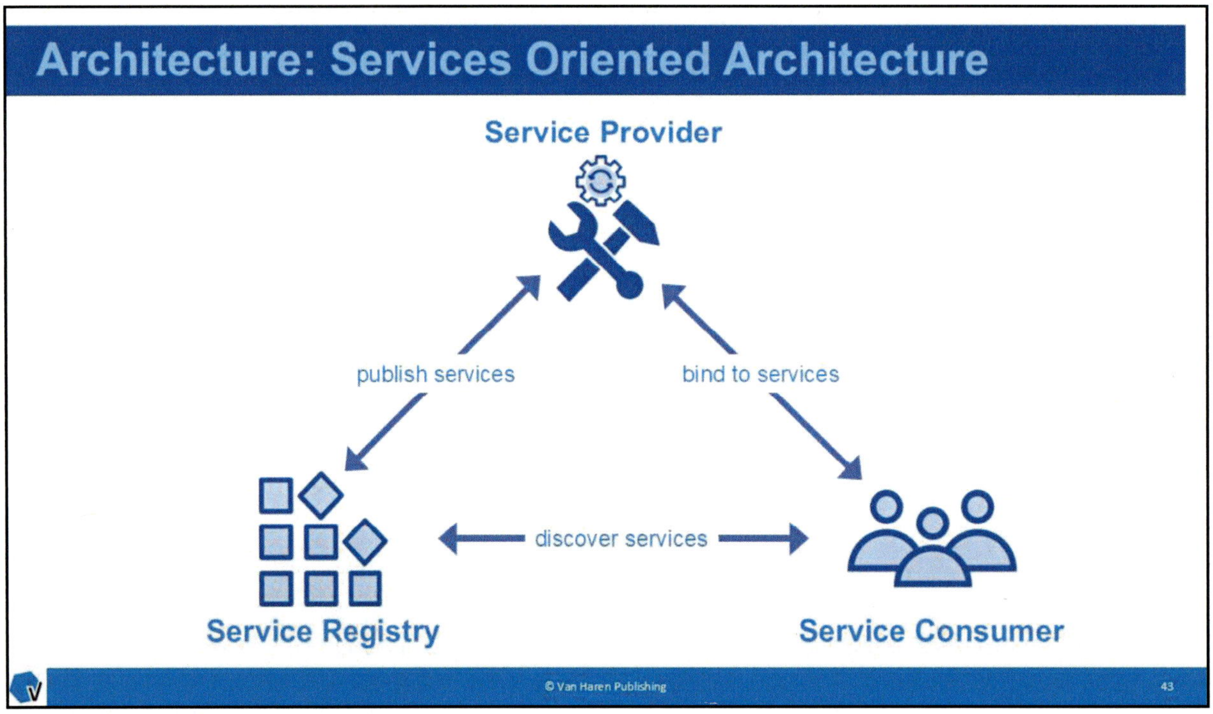
Architecture: Services Oriented Architecture
Service Provider
publish services
bind to services
discover services
Service Registry
Service Consumer
© Van Haren Publishing
43

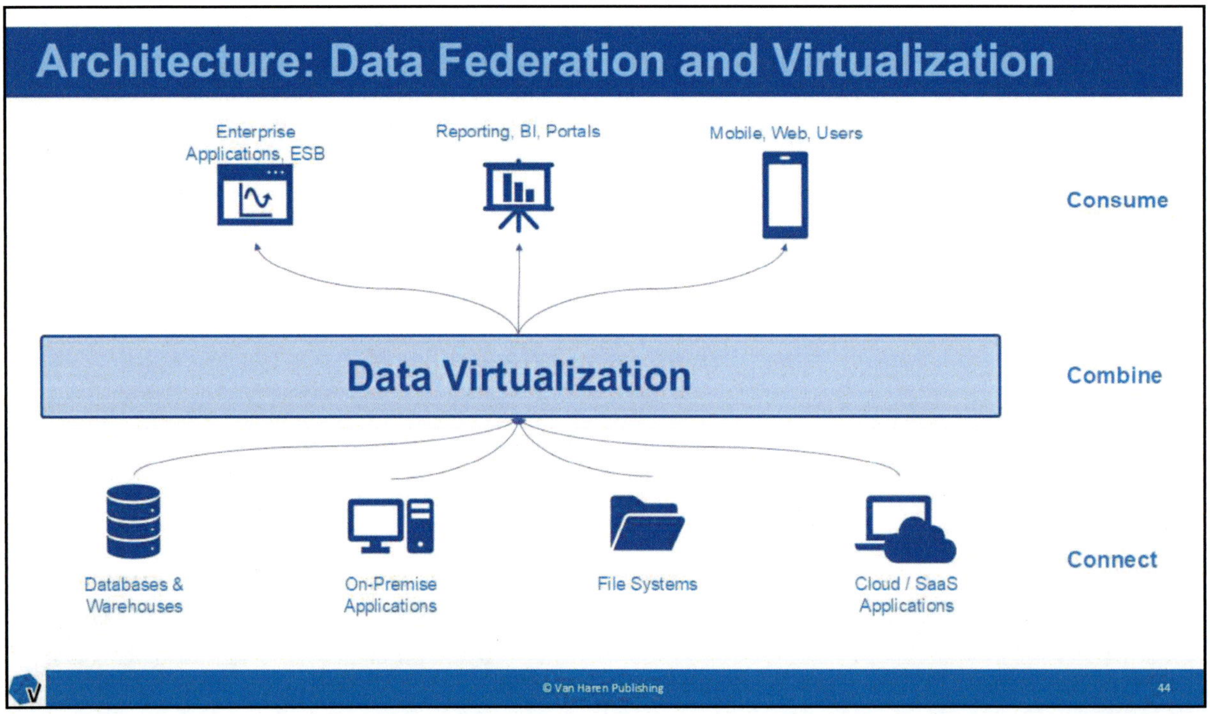
Architecture: Data Federation and Virtualization
Enterprise Applications, ESB
Reporting, BI, Portals
Mobile, Web, Users
Consume
Data Virtualization
Combine
Databases & Warehouses
On-Premise Applications
File Systems
Cloud / SaaS Applications
Connect
© Van Haren Publishing
44

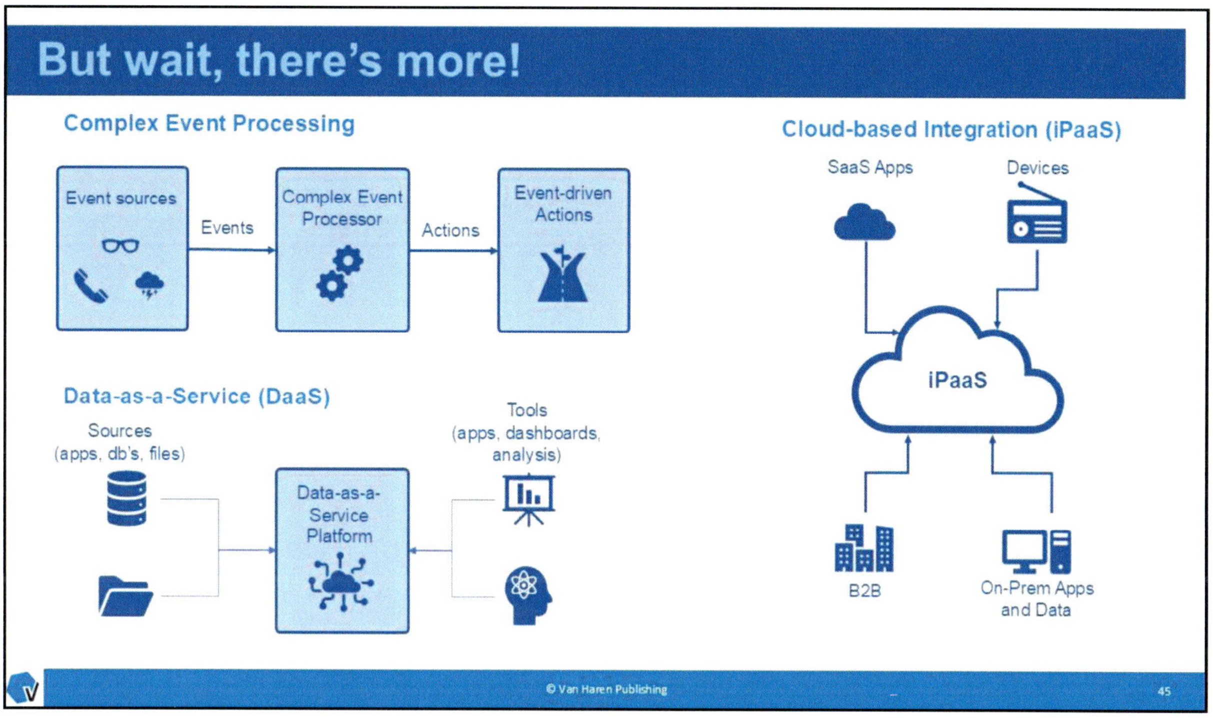
But wait, there's more!
Complex Event Processing
Event sources
Events
Complex Event Processor
Actions
Event-driven Actions
Data-as-a-Service (DaaS)
Sources
(apps, db's, files)
Data-as-a-Service Platform
Tools
(apps, dashboards, analysis)
Cloud-based Integration (iPaaS)
SaaS Apps
Devices
iPaaS
B2B
On-Prem Apps and Data
© Van Haren Publishing
45

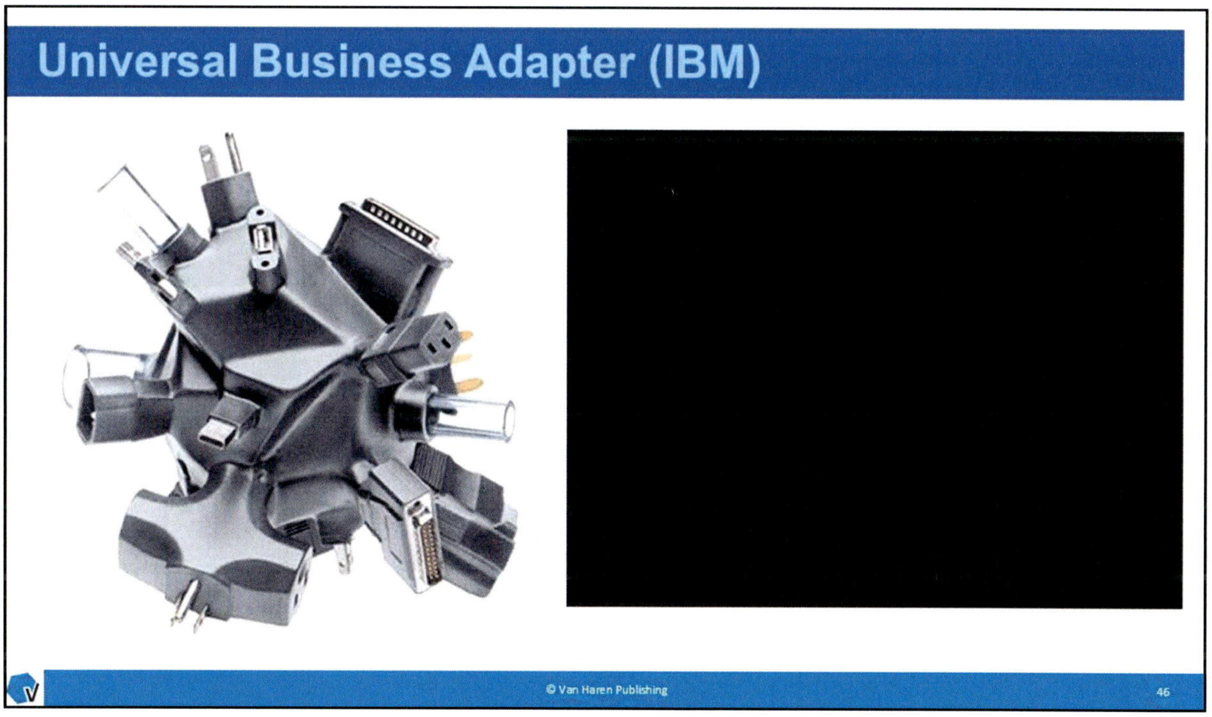
Universal Business Adapter (IBM)
© Van Haren Publishing
46

Data Exchange Standards
© Van Haren Publishing
47

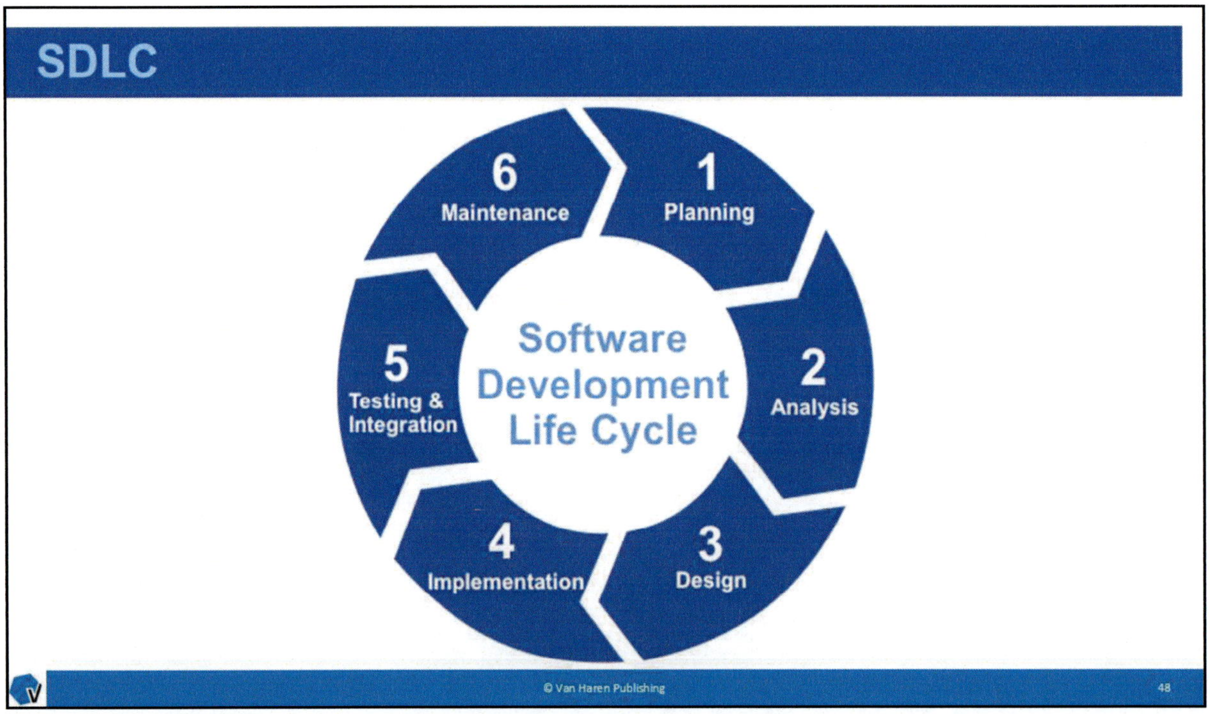
SDLC
6
Maintenance
1
Planning
Software
Development
Life Cycle
5
Testing &
Integration
2
Analysis
4
Implementation
3
Design
© Van Haren Publishing
48

Activities: Plan & Analyze

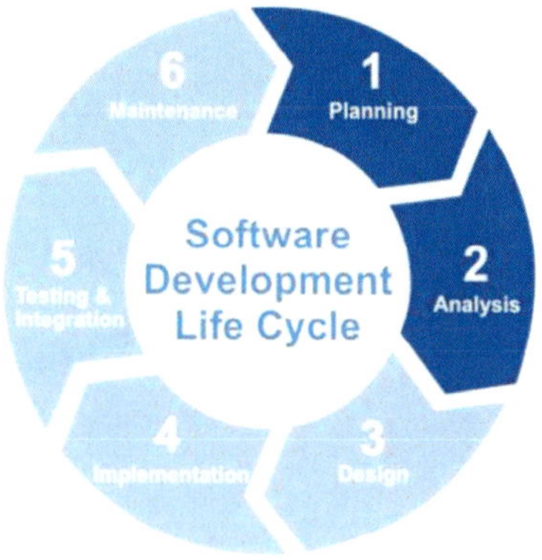

Define Data Integration and Lifecycle **Requirements**

Perform Data **Discovery**

Document **Data Lineage**

Profile Data

Collect **Business Rules**

Activities: Design

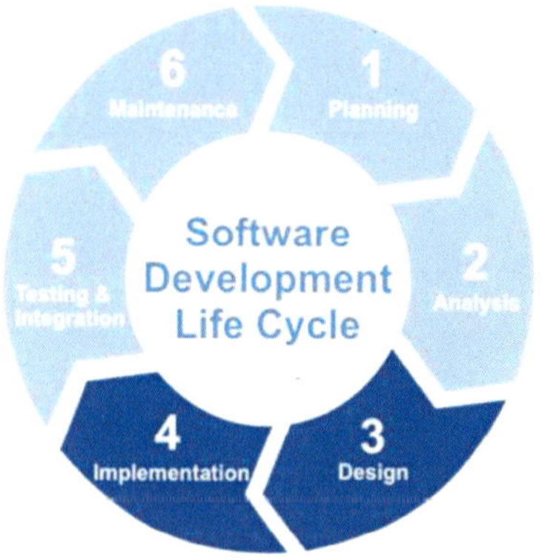

Design Data Integration **Architecture**

Model Data Hubs, Interfaces, Messages, and Data Services

Map Data Sources to Targets

Design Data **Orchestration**

Activities: Develop

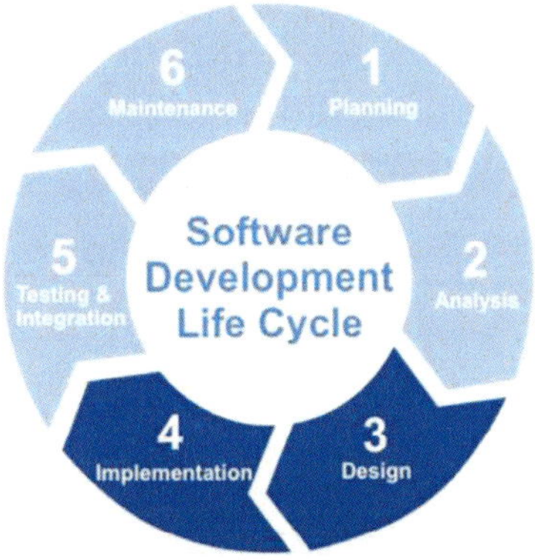

Develop Data **Services**

Develop Data **Flows**

Develop Data **Migration** Approach

Develop **Publication** Approach

Develop **Complex Event Processing** Flows

Maintain DII **Metadata**

 51

Activities: Implement and Monitor

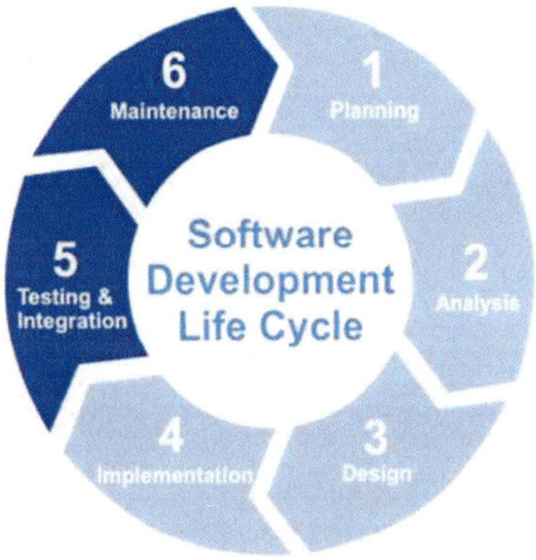

Activate data services

Real-time **monitoring** of processes

Establish parameters to indicate **potential** processing **problems**

Monitor data interaction capabilities

 52

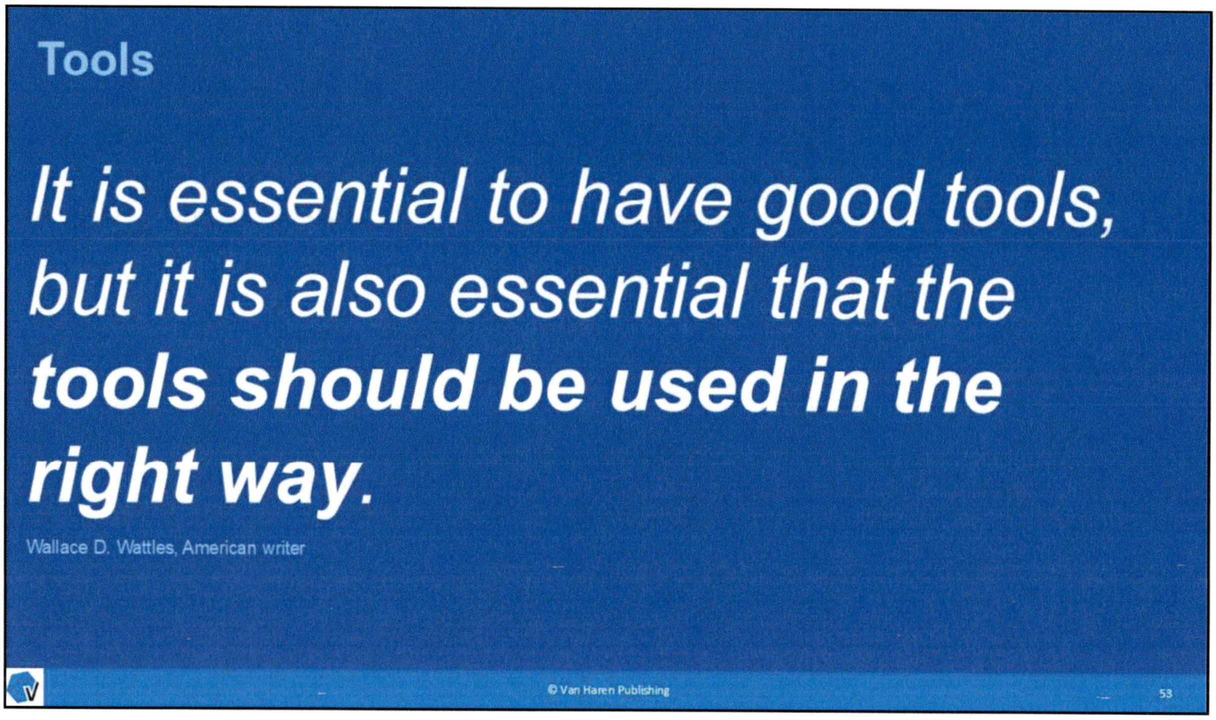
Tools
It is essential to have good tools, but it is also essential that the tools should be used in the right way.
Wallace D. Wattles, American writer
© Van Haren Publishing
53

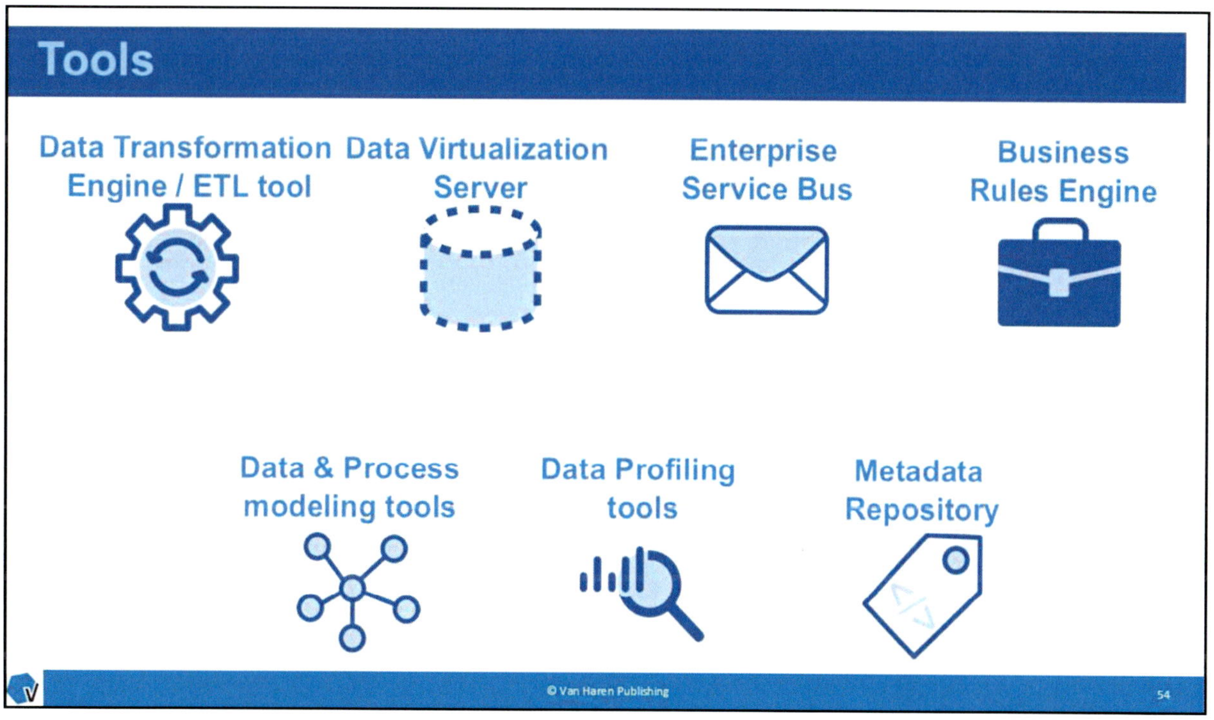
Tools
Data Transformation Engine / ETL tool
Data Virtualization Server
Enterprise Service Bus
Business Rules Engine
Data & Process modeling tools
Data Profiling tools
Metadata Repository
© Van Haren Publishing
54

Implementation guidelines
Ideas are easy
Implementation is hard
Guy Kawasaki
© Van Haren Publishing
55

Implementation guidelines
Readiness Assessment
Risk Assessment
Organization and
Cultural Change
© Van Haren Publishing
56

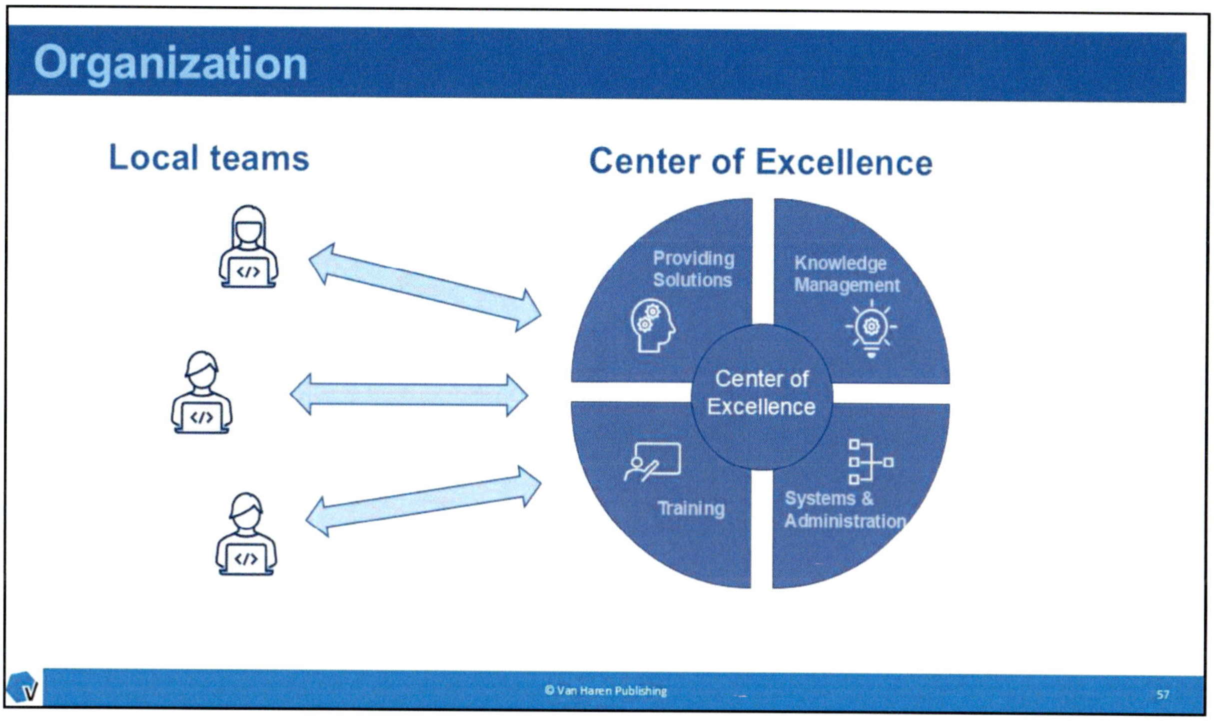
Organization
Local teams
Center of Excellence
Providing Solutions
Knowledge Management
Center of Excellence
Training
Systems & Administration
© Van Haren Publishing
57

DII Governance
BUSINESS DRIVEN DESIGN DECISIONS
CONTROLS FOR CORRECTNESS, SECURITY AND RELIABILITY
SLA'S AND BUSINESS CONTINUITY PLANS
ENTERPRISE-WIDE POLICIES
© Van Haren Publishing
58

Data Sharing Agreements

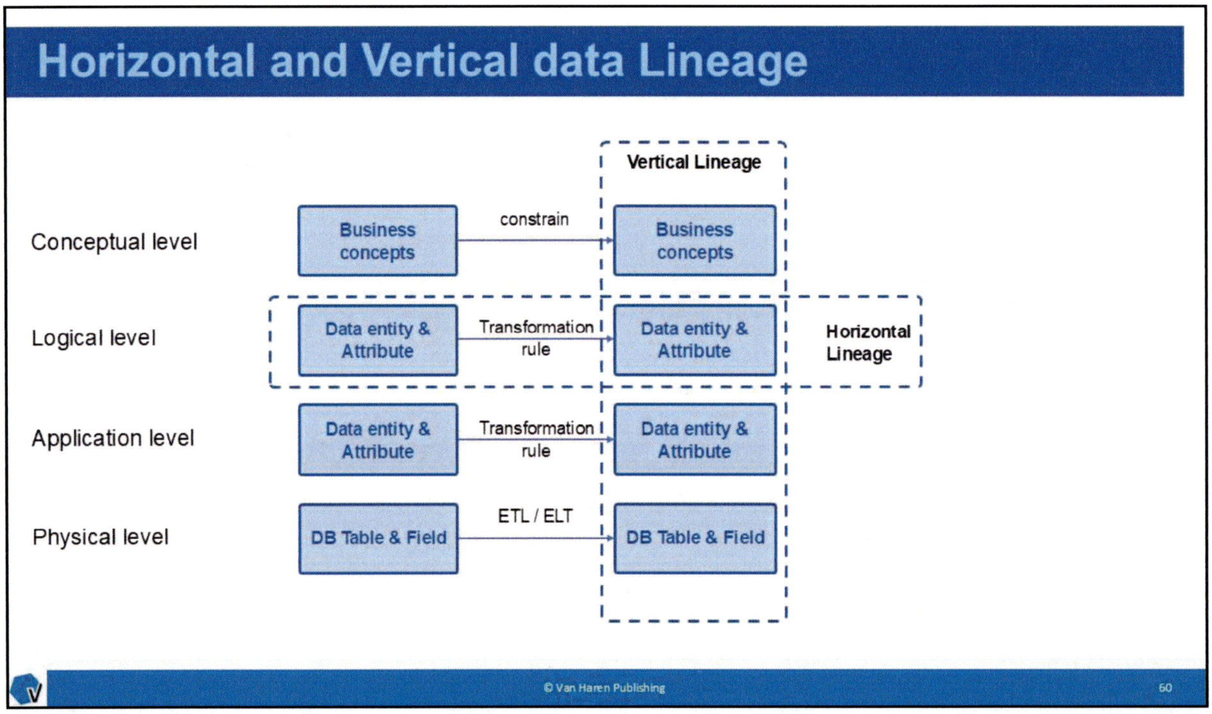
Horizontal and Vertical data Lineage
Vertical Lineage
Conceptual level
Business concepts
constrain
Business concepts
Logical level
Data entity & Attribute
Transformation rule
Data entity & Attribute
Horizontal Lineage
Application level
Data entity & Attribute
Transformation rule
Data entity & Attribute
Physical level
DB Table & Field
ETL / ELT
DB Table & Field
© Van Haren Publishing
60

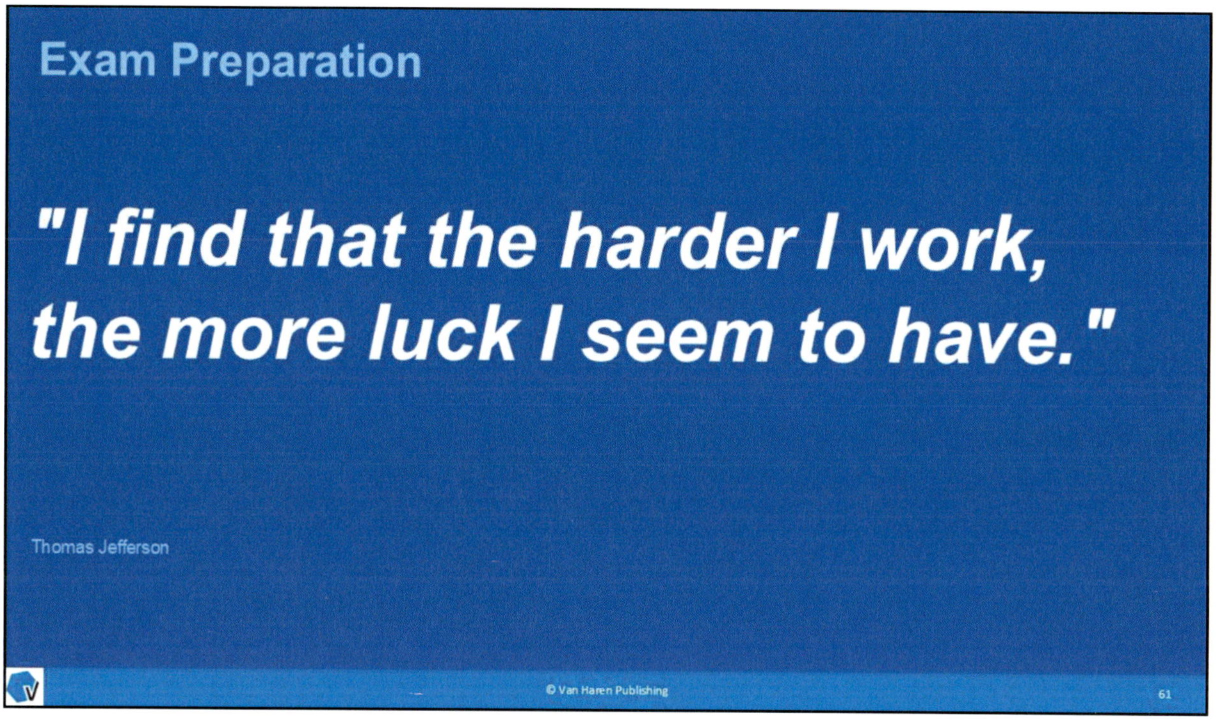
Exam Preparation
"I find that the harder I work, the more luck I seem to have."
Thomas Jefferson
© Van Haren Publishing
61

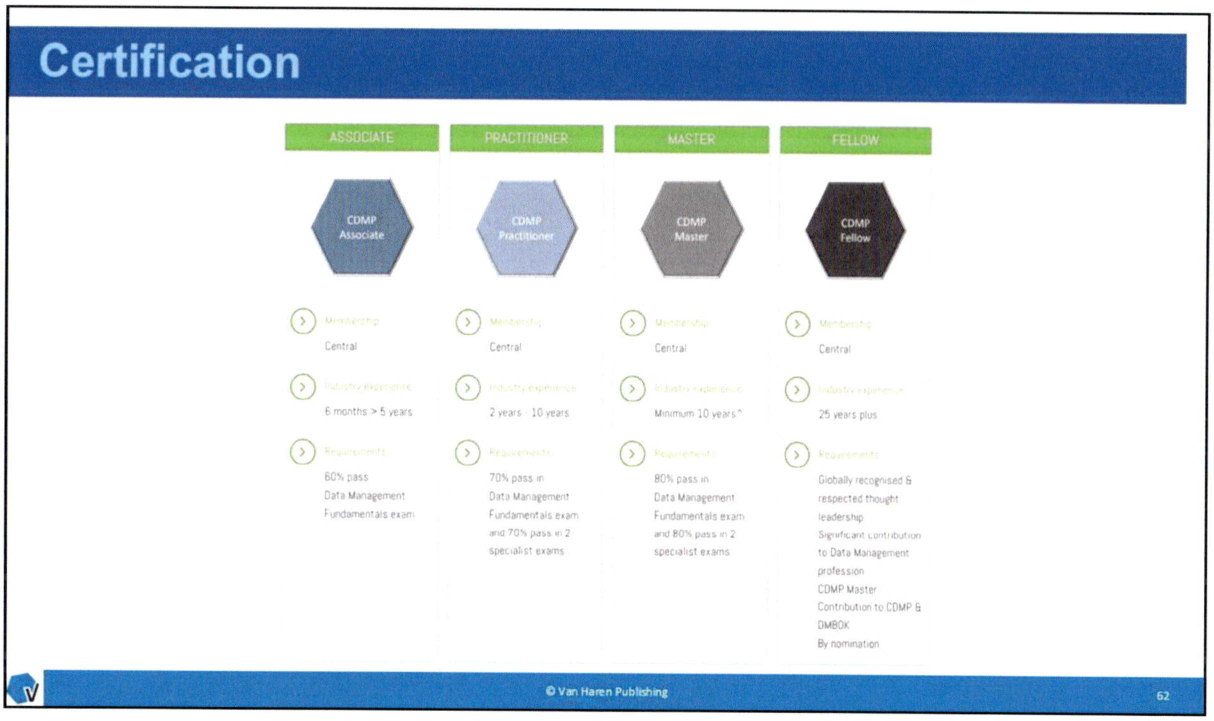
Certification
ASSOCIATE
PRACTITIONER
MASTER
FELLOW
CDMP Associate
CDMP Practitioner
CDMP Master
CDMP Fellow
Membership
Central
Industry experience
6 months > 5 years
Requirements
60% pass Data Management Fundamentals exam
Membership
Central
Industry experience
2 years - 10 years
Requirements
70% pass in Data Management Fundamentals exam and 70% pass in 2 specialist exams
Membership
Central
Industry experience
Minimum 10 years^
Requirements
80% pass in Data Management Fundamentals exam and 80% pass in 2 specialist exams
Membership
Central
Industry experience
25 years plus
Requirements
Globally recognised & respected thought leadership
Significant contribution to Data Management profession
CDMP Master
Contribution to CDMP & DMBOK
By nomination
© Van Haren Publishing
62

Example question

1. Which tool evaluates the format, completeness, consistency, validity, and structural aspects of data within data integration solutions?

A. Data and Process Modeling tools
B. Metadata Repository
C. Data Profiling Tool
D. Data Quality Assessment Solution
E. ETL (Extract, Transform, Load) Platform

 63

Example question

2. Which type of metadata is typically excluded from storage within a Metadata Repository for Data Integration Projects?

A. The organization of files on a personal computer
B. Business rules governing data transformation and lineage
C. Data schema detailing sourcing, transformation, and target structures
D. Regulatory compliance requirements for integrated data
E. Data ownership and stewardship responsibilities

 64

Example question

3. Which of the following activities does not typically fall under designing data integration solutions?

A. Design data orchestration
B. Model data hubs, interfaces, messages, and data services
C. Conduct performance testing of data integration workflows
D. Map data sources to targets
E. Design data integration architecture

 65

Example question

4. What is the primary purpose of a record management system?

A. Provide a virtual view of physically distributed data
B. Retain all data issues in a central repository
C. Retain critical business records
D. Facilitate compliance with regulatory requirements
E. Establish version control and audit trails for documents

 66

Example question

5. What is a canonical data model?

A. A model that consolidates shared data in a central data hub
B. A model that captures the high-level data requirements as a collection of related concepts
C. A model that standardizes the format in which data is shared
D. A model that focuses solely on data visualization techniques
E. A model that utilizes blockchain technology for data storage and retrieval

 67

Example question

6. Which tool often serves as both operation engines and design tool?

A. ETL tool
B. Data Modeling tool
C. Data Discovery tool
D. Customer Relationship Management (CRM) software
E. Project Management tool
F. Document Collaboration platform

 68

Example question

7. What is the main function of the transform process in data integration?

A. Generates synthetic data for testing purposes
B. Implements data governance policies
C. Make the selected data compatible with the consumer requirements
D. Encrypts the data for secure transmission
E. Automates data backup and recovery operations

Example question

8. Which of the following components is typically not a primary focus in the design of a data integration solution?

A. Exchange patterns
B. Data services
C. Data governance policies
D. Data integration architecture
E. The flow of data

Example question

9. What is the primary objective of data discovery?

A. Collect business rules
B. Identify potential sources of data
C. Optimize database performance
D. Generate synthetic data for testing purposes
E. Monitor data quality metrics

Example question

10. Which of the following is not typically considered a technology used to implement service-oriented architecture?

A. Web services
B. Messaging
C. XML
D. RESTful APIs
E. NoSQL

Example question

11. Data retention solutions (e.g., archiving) will differ depending on which factor?

A. Interaction model
B. Software licensing agreements
C. Frequency of software updates
D. Data domain and type
E. User experience

Example question

12. What is the primary characteristic of an asynchronous near real-time integration?

A. Data is processed in chunks for intermittent handling by the recipient system
B. Message integrity is verified before transmission
C. Communication between systems occurs independently of immediate response times
D. The sending and receiving applications are tightly coupled
E. The sending system does not wait for message processing by the receiving system

Example question

13. Which of the following is not a benefit of reliable Data Integration and Interoperability metadata to an organization?

A. Enhance customer satisfaction levels
B. Reduce cost
C. Replace data operations
D. Obtain more value from its data
E. Manage risks

Example question

14. Which of the following is not an activity involved in developing data integration solutions?

A. Develop business intelligence dashboards
B. Develop complex event processing flows
C. Develop data flows
D. Develop data services
E. Develop data migration approach

Example question

15. What is the role of a Data Virtualization Server?

A. Evaluate the data quality of a dataset
B. Offer a transformed and integrated perspective of the source data
C. Monitor and analyze data usage patterns
D. Implement data encryption and decryption mechanisms
E. Enhance the end-user experience through optimization

Example question - Answers

1.	C	11.	D
2.	A	12.	E
3.	C	13.	A
4.	C	14.	A
5.	C	15.	B
6.	A		
7.	C		
8.	C		
9.	B		
10.	E		

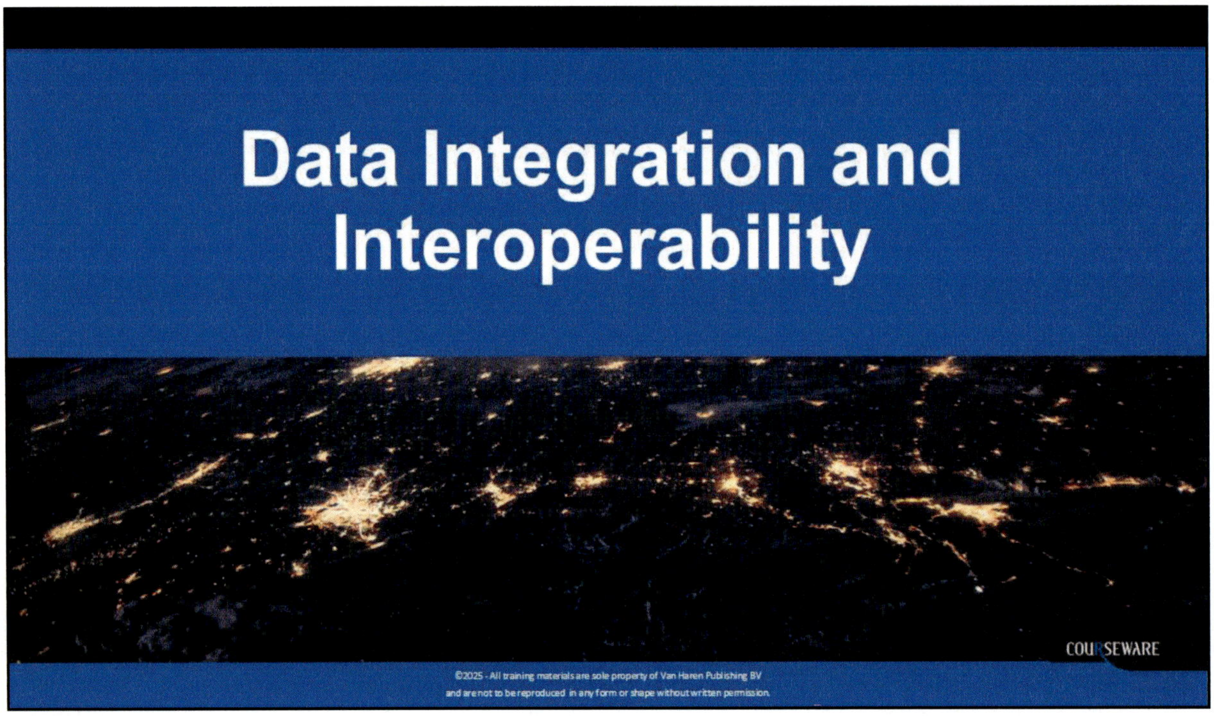
Data Integration and Interoperability
COURSEWARE
©2025 - All training materials are sole property of Van Haren Publishing BV
and are not to be reproduced in any form or shape without written permission.

Made in United States
Orlando, FL
04 November 2026

90205812R00031